STRATEGIES OF "WRITING THE SELF" IN THE FRENCH MODERN NOVEL

Back cover photo:
Portrait Palace, Willow Grove, Pennsylvania.

Strategies of "Writing the Self" in the French Modern Novel
C'est moi, je crois

Eileen M. Angelini

Studies in French Literature
Volume 52

The Edwin Mellen Press
Lewiston•Queenston•Lampeter

Library of Congress Cataloging-in-Publication Data

Angelini, Eileen M.
   Strategies of "writing the self" in the French modern novel : c'est moi, je crois / Eileen
M. Angelini.
     p. cm. -- (Studies in French Literature ; v. 52)
   Includes bibliographical references and index.
   ISBN 0-7734-7317-3
   1. Autobiographical fiction, French--History and criticism. 2. French fiction--20th
century--History and criticism. 3. Self in literature. 4. Sarraute, Nathalie. Enfance. 5
Duras, Marguerite. Amant. 6. Robbe-Grillet, Alain, 1922---Criticism and interpretation.
I. Title. II. Studies in French literature (Lewiston, N.Y.) ; v. 52.

PQ637.A96 A54 2001
843'.9109384--dc21

2001034270

This is volume 52 in the continuing series
Studies in French Literature
Volume 52 ISBN 0-7734-7317-3
SFL Series ISBN 0-88946-572-X

A CIP catalog record for this book is available from the British Library.

The Edwin Mellen Press
Box 450
Lewiston, New York
USA 14092-0450

The Edwin Mellen Press
Box 67
Queenston, Ontario
CANADA L0S 1L0

The Edwin Mellen Press, Ltd.
Lampeter, Ceredigion, Wales
UNITED KINGDOM SA48 8LT

Printed in the United States of America

For my husband, Bob O'Malley,
the love of my life,
and
for our daughter, Maureen Caroline O'Malley,
the love of our lives.

Table of Contents

Preface

"What kind of man or woman will write a book about himself?. . ." C.D.E. Tolton posed this question in his study of André Gide, and it is this question that stimulates Eileen M. Angelini's study of writing as an exploration of the self. In *Strategies of "Writing the Self": C'est moi, je crois,* in the French Modern Novel, Angelini analyzes "autofictional narratives"—i.e., fictional works into which the author has introduced elements of his or her personal life—of Nathalie Sarraute, Marguerite Duras, and Alain Robbe-Grillet. The theoretical works of Philippe Lejeune, Georges May, Gérard Genette, and others inform this study, defining autobiography, memoir, and confession, and distinguishing these forms of "writing the self" from "autofictional narrative."

Central to the autofictional narrative is the concept of "autobiographical space." While autobiography depends on retrospective narration, concealing as much about the author as it reveals, the "autofictional narrative" dispenses with the traditional single narrator. Instead, multiple narrators and characters reveal multiple levels of the author's identity. The notion of "autobiographical space" allows access to that multiplicity by bringing together in the same interpretive space several works by the same author.

In the introductory chapter of her book, Professor Angelini analyzes another key distinction between autobiography and autofictional narrative, the role of the narrator. In autobiography, the narrator is central, while in an autofictional narrative, the protagonist is central, often concealing the narrator.

The protagonist, no longer bound to recount the author's life in the circumstances in which it was lived, may adopt any of several points of view, including that of an omniscient narrator or that of the autobiographer's alter ego. The result of using these varied points of view is to give to the autofictional narrative an internal focus, rather than the external focus of autobiography.

In *Strategies of "Writing the Self": C'est moi, je crois,* in the French Modern Novel, Professor Angelini examines these multiple narrative voices in the work of three contemporary French novelists. Chapter Two studies the dialoguing voices of Nathalie Sarraute's *Enfance*, while Chapter Three presents a thorough analysis of the voices of Marguerite Duras' *L'Amant*, with its alternation of first- and third-person narration. Finally, Angelini examines the blurring of the distinction between fact and fiction in Alain Robbe-Grillet's *Romanesques* trilogy, where the author combines autobiography, fiction, and critical theory. In each instance, Angelini considers these autofictional narratives across the autobiographical space of each author's other works, and she considers such important paratextual information as interviews, where the authors talk about their intentions and other aspects of their writing.

Both paratextual information and textual metacommentary support Angelini's reading of Nathalie Sarraute's *Enfance* (1983), as she studies Sarraute's autofictional narrative in the context of both interviews with journalists and Sarraute's other works, including *Tropismes* (1939) and *L'Ère du soupçon* (1970). Indeed, the "tropisms" that guided Sarraute in both her creative and critical works are central to the reader's engagement with the dialoguing voices of *Enfance*.

In the life sciences, tropism is the responsive growth or movement of an organism toward or away from an external stimulus. For Sarraute, tropisms are things not said or movements that cross our consciousness very rapidly—a series of "pre-linguistic movements." Tropisms thus constitute the basis of everything that happens within us and that is transmitted by sensations. And it is sensations, rather than actual facts from her childhood, that Sarraute seeks to render in *Enfance*, a dialogue between the author at age 83 and "herself" as a child.

Vital to the process of rendering sensations is Sarraute's ability to listen beyond or beneath the social surface of discourse and to grasp what is really going on in the minds of her speakers. She frequently accomplishes this by lending a careful—and bilingual—ear to conversations, words, and phrases, concentrating on each syllable until it becomes palpable, no longer sliding swiftly across the consciousness of either the speaker or the reader. Thus, as Professor Angelini demonstrates, the reader of *Enfance* engages in the conversation carried on by three well-defined by overlapping first-person narrative voices and enters into a collaboration with those voices that seek to make perceptible the author's sensations of her childhood.

While Sarraute's work is characterized by "pre-linguistic movements," Marguerite Duras depends on silences and hesitations, on what is not said, to create her autofictional narratives, including *L'Amant* (1984). Sarraute's *Enfance* is informed by the uprooted nature of her childhood. (Sarraute was born in Russia and moved first to Geneva, then to Paris at the age of two, following her parents' divorce. She was then for a period of time shuttled between her father's home in Paris and her mother's home in Russia before finally settling permanently in Paris with her father and her stepmother.) In similar fashion, Duras' *L'Amant* is informed by her childhood in colonial French Indochina, a childhood surrounded by her neurotic mother, her slightly retarded younger brother—whom she adored—and her violent older brother.

As she does with *Enfance*, Angelini offers a reading of L'Amant in the context of paratextual information in the form of interviews and Duras' other autofictional narratives, especially *Un Barrage contre le Pacifique* (1950), *Des Journées entières dans les arbres* (1954), *L'Eden cinéma* (1984), and *L'Amant de la Chine du Nord* (1991). Whereas *Enfance* is organized around first-person narration, L'Amant is characterized by the presence of three alternating narrative voices. Duras' first-person authorial voice remembers her adolescence, while two distinct third-person narrators offer a second perspective on the author's adolescence and tell about the older Duras.

Professor Angelini offers a careful explication of Duras' writing strategy, in which an identification among author, narrator, and protagonist allows for changes in the narrative climate as one moves from first- to third-person narration. Shifting narrative climates and multiple levels of identity revealed by the various narrative voices demand that the reader participate in the process as Duras seeks to make sense of her life across the autobiographical space of all of her writing. And, as Angelini demonstrates, Duras employs these narrative strategies to question the nature of memory itself, even as she distances herself from the text through third-person narration and shifts the focus to points of view external to her own.

While *Enfance* and *L'Amant* are exemplars of autofictional narratives, *Le Miroir qui revient, Angélique ou l'enchantement*, and *Les Derniers jours de Corinthe*—the novels of the *Romanesques* trilogy—of Alain Robbe-Grillet represent a new genre, one that might be described as "autofiction." Robbe-Grillet goes beyond the notion of autobiographical space as he deliberately blurs the lines between fact and fiction in his work by combining fiction with elements of autobiography and critical theory. Critical theory, however, dominates the other elements, forming a metacommentary on the novels in the trilogy.

In this study, Professor Angelini examines Robbe-Grillet's strategies of "writing the self" through the fictional character of Henri de Corinthe, Robbe-Grillet's double in literature. Like Duras, Robbe-Grillet questions the nature of memory itself, as the uncertainties he encounters in trying to recount Corinthe's past parallel the uncertainties he has about recounting his own past. But to a far greater degree than either Sarraute or Duras, Robbe-Grillet examines the process of writing, continually inserting into his texts metacommentaries that focus on the way his writing develops. As in the work of Duras, the texts of Robbe-Grillet demand attentive reading and active participation on the part of the reader since these texts have a number of fragmentary elements, creating an open work with structures that are in constant movement.

All three of the authors of Angelini's study are practitioners of the "Nouveau Roman," challenging traditional conceptions of the novel. Furthermore, all three have broken with conventional autobiographical genres, creating autofictional narratives in which varied narrative voices continually shift the focus from external to internal and offer metacommentary on the text. Through her careful explication of these autofictional narratives, Professor Angelini expands our understanding of the use of new strategies of "writing the self."

Nancy M. McElveen
Greensboro College

Acknowledgments

I would like to thank the following people for their steadfast help and support with my research endeavors: my husband Bob O'Malley, my number one fan, especially for his patience with all the proofreading nightmares with my manuscript and for being a wonderful daddy to our daughter Maureen; my parents, Maureen and Joseph Angelini, who have always been loyal fans and for their extra hands when my daughter needed attention while I was revising chapters; my graduate school advisor, Inge C. Wimmers, Professor of French at Brown University, who, long after graduation, routinely continues to provide insight and wisdom on all aspects of my research; Thomas Pavel, Professor in the Department of Romance Languages and Literatures at the University of Chicago for selecting me to participate in his 1996 NEH Summer Seminar, "After Poststructuralism: The Individual in Contemporary French Thought" and for introducing me to David Bellos, Professor and Chair of the Department of Romance Languages and Literatures at Princeton University, who chose me as his Visiting Research Collaborator in 1998; Gerald Prince, Professor and Chair of the Department of Romance Languages at the University of Pennsylvania for granting me Visiting Scholar status and library privileges; my high school art teacher, Jeanne Zephir, for her creative inspiration; my dear friend, Jean L. Frick, for her faithful guidance on all my research projects; Nancy McElveen, Professor of French at Greensboro College, who graciously agreed to write the book's preface and who promptly told me that it would be an honor to do so; and, my colleagues in the School of General Studies at Philadelphia University, in particular, my office mate, Barbara A. Kimmelman, Associate Professor of History, and William R. Brown, Professor of English, who offered fresh eyes to my drafts and who repeatedly wrote letters of recommendation that enabled me to receive outside research monies. I would also like to thank my institution, Philadelphia University, which granted me a sabbatical leave for the 2000-2001 academic year so that I could complete this project and for the Faculty Research Grant Award that defrayed research expenses. Finally, a huge thank you goes to my daughter Maureen for all her delightful smiles and giggles.

Chapter One

Introduction

What kind of man or woman will write a book about himself? Is he vain? The opinion seems to be that while he may indeed be egotistical, he is more often curious -- about the kind of person he really is, and how he came to be that way. Writing, then, becomes a self-exploratory function. - C.D.E. Tolton, *André Gide and the Art of Autobiography: A Study of "Si le grain ne meurt."* [1]

The twentieth century experienced a highly varied profusion of styles of self-expression. In writing, the exploration of the self, of myriad selves, often presents a challenge to the reader. This *l'écriture de soi* or "writing the self" is not limited to the genre of autobiography, but is present in such related genres as confessions, memoirs, the intimate journal, the self-portrait and the new hybrid genre of the *récit autobiographique fictif* or "autofictional narrative" (a fictional work in which an author introduces elements of her/his personal life) that has emerged in recent years. The study of the diverse aspects of "writing the self" requires then a clear understanding of these terms and of the differences among them.

The very generality of the definition of autobiography given by Vapereau in 1876 provides contemporary theorist Philippe Lejeune with a good starting point for distinguishing the genre of autobiography from that of the "autofictional narrative." For Vapereau, autobiography is an "oeuvre littéraire, roman, poème, traité philosophique, etc., dont l'auteur a eu l'intention, secrète ou avouée, de raconter sa vie, d'exposer ses pensées ou de peindre ses sentiments."[2] He also makes a comparison with memoirs and confessions in order to demarcate clearly the specificity of autobiography. According to him, memoirs must report exact facts and confessions must attempt to retrace the truth. To be more precise, memoirs relate events in which the author participated or of which s/he was a witness; and confessions expose frankly the mistakes or errors of the author's life. The focus of memoirs is on the external world and the focus of confessions is on the inner world.

However, confessions are not only a means of exposing one's mistakes or errors; they are also a means of defending or protecting oneself. Georges May, in his book *l'Autobiographie*, clarifies the distinction to be made between autobiography and confessions/apology by using J.J. Rousseau as an example:

> L'intention autobiographique désignée par le terme d'apologie peut se définir comme le besoin d'écrire afin de justifier en public les actions qu'on a commises ou les idées qu'on a professées. Ce besoin se fait ressentir de manière particulièrement pénible et urgent *lorsqu'on a lieu de penser qu'on a été calomnié*. C'est de toute évidence le cas de Rousseau, comme il en convient lui-même dans le préambule des *Confessions* composé en 1764, donc avant même que l'obsession de la persécution eût atteint en lui son apogée: "Puisque mon nom doit durer parmi les hommes, je ne veux pas qu'il y porte une réputation mensongère; je ne veux point qu'on me donne des vertus ou des vices que je n'avais point, ni qu'on me peigne sous des traits qui ne furent pas les miens."[3]

In delineating the difference between autobiography and memoirs, Roy Pascal, in his book *Design and Truth in Autobiography*, points out that autobiography gives a report "which involves the reconstruction of the movement of a life, or part of a life, in the actual circumstances in which it was lived."[4] He places emphasis on the fact that the center of interest of an autobiography must be the self of the person who lived the described experiences rather than the exterior world, while accepting that the exterior world must appear in the work in the double role of backdrop and witness to the evolution of a personality. Memoirs, on the other hand, have another focus by presenting instead the events and persons surrounding the protagonist. This idea of "the reconstruction of the movement of a life" can be linked to the ideas of Paul Ricoeur on the narrative intelligibility of the human experience. Ricoeur writes: "... The third anchor point of the story in life lies in what one could call the *pre-narrative quality of human experience*. Thanks to it we have the right to speak of life as of an incipient story, and thus of life *as an activity and a desire in search of a narrative*."[5]

There is a further distinction to be made between autobiography and the intimate journal. May indicates that this difference is based upon the temporal gap between the event and its notation:

> C'est que l'écart entre le temps de l'expérience et celui de sa notation est plus grand dans le cas de l'autobiographie que dans celui du journal intime. Les conséquences de ce fait, même si celui-ci ne se prête pas lui-même à une mesure précise, ne laissent pas d'être considérables: au lieu d'être noté dans la fraîcheur et peut-être aussi dans la confusion de sa première impression, le souvenir a eu d'une part, le temps de reposer dans la mémoire et de s'y modifier au contact des autres souvenirs qui y ont été enregistrés avant ou depuis, et d'autre part, révèle par le fait même qu'il a survécu à l'érosion du temps que son importance le distingue hiérarchiquement de ceux qui ont sombré dans l'oubli.[6]

This temporal gap between the event and its notation is very important for the definition of autobiography since, as opposed to the intimate journal where an "unrealistic attempt" to note everything is made, an autobiography is regulated by a process of selection which constitutes its central principal. I am using the term "unrealistic attempt" to describe the writer's efforts to be complete in writing an intimate journal; the account may, of course, not be exhaustive. Furthermore, the intimate journal focuses on contemporaneous events of more or less importance to the writing subject, which may or may not entail a complete rendering of events. In contrast, in an autobiography, it is the presence of choice of memories and their eventual selection that is characteristic of the adult or mature point of view. This choice entails an inherent tendency on the part of the autobiographer to conceal as much as s/he reveals. Moreover, in examining an autobiography, one must bear in mind the fluid nature of memory: its accuracy and/or its limitations. Essentially, the autobiographer's point of view may have greatly changed since the time of the experiences being described, a point of view that may even be a result of what was learned from the experience. For example, Marguerite Duras writes and rewrites the same memories at various points in her life as a means of gradually recovering her past. She claims: "On croit que la vie se déroule comme une route entre deux bornes, début et fin. Comme un livre qu'on en ferait. Que la vie, c'est la chronologie. C'est faux. Tandis qu'on est à vivre un événement, on l'ignore. C'est par la mémoire, ensuite, qu'on croit savoir ce qu'il y a eu."[7] For her, the role of memory is essential since it will alter the selection process, especially as one age, has had more time to reflect, and the pain of trauma has eased. In the chapter on Duras, a detailed analysis of this technique is presented.

In distinguishing between autobiography and self-portrait, Michel Beaujour in his book, *Miroirs d'encre: rhétorique de l'autoportrait*, argues that the self-portrait "se distingue de l'autobiographie par l'absence d'un récit suivi."[8] According to Beaujour, since the self-portrait lacks a "continous narrative," its main emphasis is its organization around a thematic or logical principle. However, he further asserts that the operating formula of a self-portrait is: "Je ne vous raconterai pas ce que j'ai fait, mais je vais vous dire *qui je suis*."[9] Consequently, for Beaujour, a self-portrait is a description of the author at the actual time of her/his writing and is written in the present tense. The self-portrait is not a description of past events; although, past events may be evoked in order to better explain the present state of the author.

A more current definition of autobiography than that of Vapereau is the definition given by Lejeune in his book *l'Autobiographie en France*. Lejeune defines autobiography as follows: "le récit rétrospectif en prose que quelqu'un fait de sa propre existence quand il met l'accent principal sur l'histoire de sa personnalité."[10] Lejeune, consequently, eliminates poetry from his definition of autobiography. He also eliminates memoirs because their principal perspective is not centered on the history or the evolution of the protagonist's personality. Furthermore, he does not include the intimate journal since it is not, according to him, a "retrospective narrative." This notion of a retrospective narrative is a key notion for the definition of the genre of autobiography as it underlines the importance of the dimension of the temporal gap between the event and its notation. The three authors that are the focus of this study, Nathalie Sarraute, Marguerite Duras, and Alain Robbe-Grillet, break many of these rules. It is, therefore, important to examine how their works affect our concept of autobiography.

Lejeune's initial definition excludes all fiction -- even the "autofictional narrative." It is not until 1975 when he writes *Le Pacte autobiographique*, a revision of *l'Autobiographie en France*, that he expands his study of autobiography by insisting on the need to define a logically antecedent *pacte autobiographique* or "autobiographical pact" ("Pourqu'il y ait autobiographie il doit y avoir une identité entre l'auteur, le narrateur, le personnage.")[11] and by introducing the key concept of *espace autobiographique* or "autobiographical space." Lejeune introduced this concept in his chapter on André Gide, since he realized that he was unable to account for the fact that Gide produced a more compelling and complex image of the self in his fictional works than in his autobiographical texts. Starting with an analysis of Gide's writing, Lejeune defines his concept of "autobiographical space" in the following manner: "Il ne s'agit pas là de ce qu'on appelle banalement une 'inspiration autobiographique,' l'écrivain utilisant des matériaux empruntés à sa vie, mais d'une stratégie visant à constituer la personnalité à travers les jeux les plus divers de l'écriture."[12] He maintains that an identity is strictly delimited in an autobiography whereas in an "autobiographical space," one is able to show multiple levels of an identity by means of a diversity of narrators and characters:

> Il est évident que c'est le régime de la fiction qui est le plus propice au libre développement des contraires et des "dissemblances". Gide se sent alors libre de pousser tour à tour à l'extrême, dans des sortes d'*essais* de lui-même, chacune des virtualités de son être: liberté vis-à-vis du lecteur, -- mais aussi libération de soi-même. La fiction devient *à la fois* confidence personnelle (quant au germe des attitudes décrites) et dépersonnalisation (quant à l'excessive ou exclusive réalisation de ce trait particulier), *à la fois* souvenir et expérimentation, *à la fois* narcissisme et autocritique. Le régime de la fiction est souvent présenté par Gide sur le mode d'une hygiène, d'une *purge* qui lui permet à la fois de s'accomplir et de se débarrasser de lui-même. Il éprouve grande volupté à ces exercices qui lui permettent de dire "je" sur le mode de l'hypothèse, de la virtualité, sans tomber dans le "moi" autobiographiques.[13]

Using the notion of "autobiographical space," it is thus possible to evaluate and to consider a wider range of possible writing strategies in autobiographical narratives, including fictional ones. It is these strategies that constitute what I define as "writing the self" -- writing that includes straightforward as well as fictional accounts -- since the concept of "autobiographical space" encompasses the image of the self across many genres or across all the works of an author.

Lejeune's concept of "autobiographical space" works equally well in examining the recent works by Nathalie Sarraute, Marguerite Duras, and Alain Robbe-Grillet, since these writers have all written texts that expand the practice of "writing the self." All three of these authors have written hybrid or multifaceted texts in which they examine their personal existence, their activities as writers and certain aspects of the society around them. These authors, associated with the *Nouveau Roman* of the second half of the twentieth century, have all used radical writing strategies. Merle Rubin explains: "The idea behind the 'new novel' was to dispense with traditional devices such as narrator, narrative, characters, and plot in order to be able to concentrate on aspects of consciousness and experience too subtle, subjective, or otherwise obscure to have received close attention in more conventional novels."[14] It now remains to be explored how these novelists developed new techniques in their "autofictional narratives." Michael Sheringham, in his article on recent strategies in new French autobiography, singles out three main tendencies: "First, the desire to circumvent the teleological properties of narrative, and its complicity with a *causal* vision of human reality: fragmentation and complexities of narrative voice are employed in this struggle. Second, the boundaries between fiction and fact, invention and recollection are contested: fiction is seen to infiltrate self-consciousness, and subjective factors to exert pressure on or in the creation of fictions. Third, the execution and justification of writing autobiography is scrutinized and commented on in detail."[15] Attentive to these radical writing strategies, I examine how the principles of the concept of "autobiographical space," which by definition entails the most diverse writing strategies to construct the personality, helps us to understand better the texts of Nathalie Sarraute, Marguerite Duras, and Alain Robbe-Grillet.

The concept of "autobiographical space" is a hermeneutical concept that brings together in the same interpretive space several texts of the author in question. It is closely linked to the concept of intertextuality, since, in both "reading takes place against a backdrop of something already said or written."[16] The reader must be aware of more than one of an author's texts since, for example, the reading of an autobiography may very well influence the reading of an "autofictional narrative" by the same writer and vice versa. Such intertextual readings within an "autobiographical space" call for an extended definition of intertextuality.[17] Comparing an autobiography and "autofictional narrative" by one and the same author can be illuminating. It shows us, for instance, the necessary distinction to be made between the hero/protagonist and the narrator. Pascal Ifri's distinction between *l'Immoraliste*, an "autofictional narrative," and *Si le grain ne meurt*, Gide's autobiography is noteworthy.[18] Ifri argues that there is a difference on the level of focalization (to use Gérard Genette's expression), that is to say, the choice or not of a restricted point of view,[19] between these two works. While according to his "autobiographical pact," Lejeune upholds that it is the author who maintains and affirms the identity among the author, the narrator, and the character, Ifri proposes the following distinction: in an autobiography, it is the narrator who is at the center of the scene; and in an "autofictional narrative," it is the hero/protagonist who occupies the central focus, since the narrator hides behind the protagonist. When an autobiographer strays from his own field of knowledge, he is obligated to properly document his sources.[20] On the other hand, the hero/protagonist of a novel can be seen from the exterior perspective of several characters who are easily manipulated by the author. Roy Pascal sums up this situation concisely when he states: "The autobiographer can neither get inside other people nor outside himself."[21]

With the concept of "autobiographical space," it is possible to enlarge the field to include at the same time fact and fiction, which, consequently, gives the author a greater choice of points of view via a diversity of narrators and characters. Along with a diversity of narrators, comes a diversity of functions of the narrator. Genette enumerates five basic functions of the narrator: 1.) Narrative: to tell the narrative or story; 2.) Organizing: to manage the narrative text and its internal organization; 3.) Communicative: to communicate directly with the narratee; 4.) "Emotive" or testimonial: the narrator reveals her/his attitude towards the story being told; and 5.) Ideological: the narrator interprets, explains, or justifies context, events, and characters via didactic discourse. This list of the narrator's five basic functions by Genette is by no means exhaustive and he readily concedes that it is only a base upon which to expand.[21]

The choice of a point of view is an integral part of the narrative situation. According to Genette, it is the choice of a point of view and the choice of voice that makes up the narrative situation. A narrative is able to communicate to us what is recounted in three different ways: 1.) a non-focalized narrative (a narrative with an omniscient narrator); 2.) a narrative with an internal focus (a limited focus); and 3.) a narrative with an external focus (a limited focus as well).[22] In a non-focalized narrative with an omniscient narrator, the narrator knows more than the characters; s/he has a more global viewpoint than they do and is consequently able to shift from one period to another, from one place to another. This type of narrative is characterized by commentaries, explanations, (restorative information), and prolepses (anticipations). In a narrative with an internal focus, the narrator fades into the background and only says what a character or the characters know. The narrator cannot intervene in order to comment, explain, fill in gaps of information, anticipate, or forewarn. The narrator has the same amount of knowledge or ignorance as do the characters and only gives to the reader the world as seen by the characters. In a narrative with an external focus, the reader is given an exterior view of a character or a scene, without being shown the thoughts or feelings of the characters. Everything is seen from a certain distance or from a vantage point of someone who is not initiated or "in the know." Of course, a narrator is able to change his/her point of view or focus. Too abrupt a change is felt by the reader as an infraction of the point of view previously established by the context. This is the case when there is an excess of information ("paralepse") or when we are given less information than is, in principle, necessary ("paralipse"). Because of the greater diversity of points of view in an "autofictional narrative," this study carefully examines the different ways of introducing narrative modes for presenting consciousness in fact and fiction.

Interesting to note is Dorrit Cohn's perspective on the three types of presentation of consciousness which can be identified in the context of third-person narration: "1. psycho-narration: the narrator's discourse about a character's consciousness; 2. quoted monologue: a character's mental discourse; 3. narrated monologue: a character's mental discourse in the guise of the narrator's discourse."[23] Of these three techniques, narrated monologue is the most linguistically complex since it keeps the third-person reference and the same narrative tense, but like the quoted monologue, it repeats verbatim the character's own mental language.

Narrated monologue thus creates an intentional hybrid.

Another important aspect of the choice of point of view that has been put forth by Cohn is the lack of attention in literary criticism to autobiographical narrators who communicate their own past inner lives. She asserts: "*retro*spection into a consciousness, though less 'magical,' is no less important a component of first-person novels than *in*spection of a consciousness is in third-person novels."[24] Although the same basic types of presentation of consciousness occur in autobiographical first-person narration as they do in third-person narration (with prefix modifications to indicate the change in relationship between the narrator and her/his subject, i.e. self-narration in place of psycho-narration and self-quoted or self-narrated for monologue), she warns that there is a definite change in narrative climate as one moves between third-person narration and autobiographical first-person narration:

> It stems from the altered relationship between the narrator and his protagonist when that protagonist is his own past self. The narration of inner events is far more strongly affected by this change of person than the narration of outer events; past thought must now be presented as *remembered* by the self, as well as expressed by the self (i.e., subject to what David Goldknopf calls the "confessional increment"). All this substantially alters the function of the three basic techniques in autobiographical narration.[25]

Equally important therefore is the need to examine the use of an alter ego or a narrator's double by an autobiographer. In presenting an alter ego, an autobiographer is able to distance himself from the text and present another side of his personality; and in so doing, the autobiographer will use different methods to introduce different voices.[26] The choice of speech type is essential to the desired point of view. As it is the combination of point of view and voice that makes up the narrative situation, the choice of speech type will have an impact on the choice of a point of view and vice versa. Boris Uspensky elucidates: "Change in the authorial point of view becomes evident in the intrusion within the authorial text of elements of someone else's speech - that is, elements of speech characteristic of one or another character. The inclusion of elements of someone else's speech is a basic device of expressing changes of point of view on the level of phraseology (or on the level of speech characteristics)."[27] Particularly striking, for example, is the speech of the character of Henri de Corinthe in *Le Miroir qui revient, Angélique ou l'enchantement*, and *Les Derniers jours de Corinthe* by Alain Robbe-Grillet. This character, who becomes the alter ego, the double in literature, of Robbe-Grillet, represents a multiplication of the narrative voice as well as a means for the author to delve into the imaginary. In a number of detailed interviews, Robbe-Grillet claims, with a direct allusion to Lejeune's "autobiographical pact": "J'ai formulé un pacte nouveau. C'est l'imaginaire qui parle; l'imaginaire qui parle du souvenir."[28] It seems that in order to account for the complex narrative of *Le Miroir qui revient*, which, according to Robbe-Grillet himself does not always respect the "autobiographical pact" as defined by Lejeune, one must enlarge Lejeune's definition in order to include not only the identity among the author, the narrator, the protagonist, which Lejeune's definition requires, but also the imaginary double(s) of protagonist/narrator/author. In the chapter on Robbe-Grillet, I will explore how Henri de Corinthe's role becomes more complex as the *Romanesques* series progresses from *Le Miroir qui revient* to *Angélique ou l'enchantement* and to *Les Derniers jours de Corinthe* since, in the second and third texts, he is allowed to speak directly for himself through first-person narration.

An analogue to Henri de Corinthe is found in *L'Amant* by Marguerite Duras. *L'Amant* is characterized by a first-person narrative of a female voice which alternates with two types of third-person narration. The three types of narration in *L'Amant* are: 1.) the first-person narration by Duras, the author-identified narrator, remembering her adolescence; 2.) the third-person narration of Duras' adolescence as seen by the omniscient narrator; and 3.) the third-person narration of the older Duras as seen by the omniscient narrator. This technique employed by Duras provides her with the means for distancing herself from her text. She is able to examine herself from an external perspective since she looks at herself as if she were another. The chapter devoted to Duras will begin with a discussion on the importance of the alternation among these three types of narration. Nathalie Sarraute also uses the technique of several voices in *Enfance*. For instance, the main function of the voice of the alter ego is to question the memory process by the voice of the author-narrator trying to remember. The chapter dedicated to Sarraute's *Enfance* provides a detailed evaluation of the role and multiple functions of the voice of the alter ego.

The problematic status of fact and fiction must also be taken into account in the refinement of the definition of "autobiographical space." In this respect, the work of Joseph Margolis is illuminating. According to Margolis, fictional worlds are not isolated from the actual world since "we can never, in practice or principle, free the features of a fictional world from *some* conceptual dependence (however limited and indeterminate it may be) on the conditions of coherence, the causal order, and the normal features of the phenomena of what we regard as the actual world."[29] The reader aspires to distinguish between that which really existed in the author's life, that which the author thought existed, and that which the author invented. This problematic status of fact and fiction explains in large part the reasons why a reader could have trouble differentiating an autobiography from an "autofictional narrative" and why an author is able to experiment with both autobiography and "autofictional narrative" while s/he attempts to incorporate the multiple levels of identity. For example, in his article "The Proustian Paratexte," Gérard Genette discusses the problematic status of dreams in Marcel Proust's *À la recherche du temps perdu.* Genette explains: "The 'hero' of my dreams who dreams them and then speaks about them in the first person, is certainly me. Then again, it isn't me. I haven't lived that dream. But, in any case, I cannot say that it is another. And in many ways, under many headings, the *Recherche* is a dreamed autobiography."[30] Genette not only concludes that *À la recherche du temps perdu* situates itself between autobiography and fiction but he also shows how Proust mixes fact and fiction in order to analyze the multiple levels of awareness and identity.

By expanding the concept of "autobiographical space," this study of the works of Sarraute, Duras, and Robbe-Grillet also includes the function of paratextual information, information that is outside the narrative text but on the topic of the narrative text in question. Particularly noteworthy are interviews of an author since they may contain information which could affect the reader's interpretation of a particular author's work. Genette, who defines "paratexte" as consisting of all the supplementary information surrounding a text, makes a key distinction between the terms "*interview*" and "*entretien*": "j'appellerai *interview* un dialogue, généralement bref et assuré par un journaliste professionnel, commis d'office à l'occasion ponctuelle de la sortie d'un livre, et portant en principe exclusivement sur ce livre; et *entretien* un dialogue généralement plus étendu, à échéance plus tardive, ... souvent assuré par un médiateur moins interchangeable, plus 'personnalisé', plus spécifiquement intéressé à l'oeuvre en cause, ..."[31]   In this study of the influence of paratextual information on the concept of "autobiographical space," I follow this distinction made by Genette and refer to *interview* as an "interview" and *entretien* as a "detailed interview."

Detailed interviews are important because it is there that authors talk about their intentions and about different aspects of their work. This information will certainly influence the reader's reception of a work; for example, if an author states that a given work is fictional but contains a number of autobiographical elements, the reader is likely to look for correspondences between the life of the author and that of the hero/protagonist of her/his "autofictional narrative." For example, in a detailed interview with Viviane Forrester, Nathalie Sarraute maintains that *Enfance* is not her autobiography since it is not a report on her entire life nor even a report on all of her childhood. She explains that it is more important for her to render the sensations rather than the events of her childhood. In the light of this explanation, *Enfance* appears to be a continuation of her research on *tropismes* or "tropisms."[32] This information constitutes an important "paratexte," since the reader is thus made aware of the author's intentions.

Finally, metacommentaries, commentaries that are found in the text and which call attention to the status of the text in question, play an important part in the works of Robbe-Grillet, Sarraute, and Duras. Metacommentaries are a part of non-narrative discourse and function on the level of *énonciation*. This level includes all the diverse commentaries of the narrator (for example, references to her/himself and his activities as a narrator, judgments, explanations, or general observations about the work in question), and sometimes even the narrator's or author's "dialogues" with the reader. For example, in *Le Miroir qui revient*, Robbe-Grillet writes:

> Pourtant, j'éprouve aujourd'hui un certain plaisir à utiliser la forme traditionnelle de l'autobiographie: cette facilité dont parle Stendhal dans ses *Souvenirs d'égotisme*, comparée à la résistance du matériau qui caractérise toute création. Et ce plaisir douteux m'intéresse dans la mesure où, d'une part, il me confirme que je me serais mis à écrire des romans pour exorciser ces fantômes dont je ne venais pas à bout, et me fait d'autre part découvrir que le biais de la fiction est, en fin de compte, beaucoup plus *personnel* que la prétendue sincérité de l'aveu.[33]

This commentary is metatextual because Robbe-Grillet talks about the type of text he is in the process of writing. The author gives a critique of his own method while sketching out a definition surprisingly close to Lejeune's notion of "autobiographical space." Sarraute introduces the voice of the alter ego that repeatedly questions or puts into question the voice of the author-narrator's autobiographical project. For example, when the voice of the author-narrator trying to remember is describing the mother's indifference when she was sick as a child, the response of the voice of the alter ego is: "– Sois juste, il lui est arrivé pendant cette maladie de venir s'asseoir près de ton lit avec un livre."[34] The function here of the voice of the alter ego is to scrutinize and verify what the other voice has recounted; that is to say, it is questioning the memory process of this voice. As a result of this questioning process by the voice of the alter ego, Sarraute is able to highlight the problems that arise from the temporal gap between an event and its notation. Duras' metacommentaries are just as important as the metacommentaries made by Robbe-Grillet and Sarraute since they reveal her conscious awareness of the nature of the autobiographical writing process. For example, when describing a photograph of her son when he was twenty and in California with his friends, Duras breaks the first-person narration to comment: "C'est cette photographie qui est au plus près de celle qui n'a pas été faite de la jeune fille du bac."[35] This metacommentary is in reference to the imaginary photograph that served as the creative catalyst for Duras' ability to write *L'Amant*.[36] It demonstrates how Duras will repeatedly refer to this imaginary photograph in order to highlight its importance in her autobiographical writing. These examples of metacommentary are further evidence that the concept of "autobiographical space" needs to be expanded to include these authors' varied modes of self-examination and expression. These metacommentaries also help readers to better understand the author's intentions and prompt them to adopt certain reading strategies. In each chapter, a full analysis of Robbe-Grillet's, Sarraute's, and Duras' frequent and prominent use of metacommentaries and their crucial role in the development of the narrative is discussed.

In more ways than one, it is necessary to enlarge Lejeune's notion of "autobiographical space," since these three new novelists have developed new techniques in their "autofictional narratives." In cultivating the new techniques, these authors break many of the rules of the genre of autobiography and consequently reshape our concept of this genre. To be kept in mind while analyzing these authors' works are the concept of intertextuality, unexpected slips in the narrative situation, the introduction of doubles or alter egos, the problematic status of fact and fiction, the function of paratextual information, and metacommentaries made by the author. The first text to be examined in this study is *Enfance* by Nathalie Sarraute. The main focus of this chapter will be on the dialoguing voices. In the next chapter, the use of a first-person narration that alternates with two distinct types of third-person narration in *L'Amant* by Marguerite Duras is central to the analysis. Also to be looked at is the role of *L'Amant* in relation to Duras' other "autofictional narratives." The focus of the following chapter is on how Alain Robbe-Grillet intentionally blurs the distinction between fact and fiction by combining autobiographical elements with fictitious elements and critical theories in *Le Miroir qui revient, Angélique ou l'enchantement,* and *Les Derniers jours de Corinthe,* his *Romanesques* trilogy. On a final important note, given the highly innovative nature of Sarraute's, Duras', and Robbe-Grillet's works, all textual quotes have been reproduced as faithfully as possible as to how they appear in the original text.

Chapter Two

Nathalie Sarraute's *Enfance*

Nathalie Sarraute a une vision protoplasmique de notre univers intérieur: ôtez la pierre du lieu commun, vous trouverez des coulées, des baves, des mucus, des mouvements hésitants, amiboïdes. Son vocabulaire est d'une richesse incomparable pour suggérer les lentes reptations centrifuges de ces élixirs visqueux et vivants. - Jean-Paul Sartre, Preface to *Portrait d'un inconnu.*[37]

In 1983, the eighty-three-year-old Nathalie Sarraute published *Enfance*, her first best-seller. Coincidentally, though the author of numerous earlier novels, this is the first work in which she openly uses autobiographical events. Sarraute, who had not begun publishing until the age of thirty-two, is a writer who has always been known as intellectual, private, and solitary, accessible only to the academic elite.

Although Sarraute claims that *Enfance* is not a report on her entire life nor even a report on all of her childhood, it merits special attention since it is considered by most critics as an autobiography. To Sarraute, rather, it is an account of selected moments whose sensation she is trying to recapture before they are lost forever, a practice central to all her works. In a detailed interview with Viviane Forrester, the novelist gave convincing reasons supporting her claims about *Enfance*:

> Ce n'est pas un rapport sur ma vie. ... Le souvenir, lorsqu'il n'est pas repris dans le travail est tellement grossier. J'ai sélectionné, comme pour tous mes autres livres, des instants dont je pourrais retrouver la sensation. Cette fois, j'ai dit qu'il s'agissait de moi, non pas d'il ou d'elle. D'où une impression d'impudeur parfois ... Non, j'ai vraiment choisi certains moments, comme toujours, proches de mon travail, de ma recherche, de mon écriture. ... Il ne s'agit pas d'un rapport sur toute ma vie. Pas même sur toute l'enfance.[38]

The most important objective for Sarraute is to render the *sensations* rather than the events from her childhood. She claims not to believe in autobiography per se because, as she explained to Jason Weiss, in every book an author will include many experiences, lived or imagined. When then questioned about there being a mistrust of autobiography, Sarraute answered:

> There is always a mise-en-scène, a desire to show oneself in a certain light. We are so complex and we have so many facets that what interests me in an autobiography is what the author wants me to see. He wants me to see him like that. That's what amuses me. And it's always false. I don't like Freud at all and I detest psychoanalysis, but one of Freud's statements I have always found very interesting, and true, is when he said that all autobiographies are false. Obviously, because I can do an autobiography that will show a saint, a being who is absolutely idyllic, and I could do another that will be a demon, and it will all be true. Because it's all mixed together. And in addition, one can't even attain all that.[39]

Sarraute is unyielding about her mistrust of autobiographies. In a detailed interview with Alfred Cismaru, she actually mocks autobiographies, with the sole exception of Rousseau's *Confessions* which she does find to be outstanding:

Gide's *Journal* is below Gide. In general I like the works of Michel
Leiris, but if it is true that he wanted to say everything in his
autobiography, he was wrong before he started. There are things
about all of us that we would rather not examine too closely, let alone
expose. There is the unsayable. As for Sartre's *Les Mots*, it is a
beautiful construction, but probably not very close to reality. It is
Sartre the intellectual, at age 59, trying to trace the intellectual
development of baby Sartre. It is phony. There is only one instance
in which I agree with Freud, and that is when he said that every
autobiography is phony.[40]

Sarraute believes that it is impossible for an adult to fully recall and accurately narrate a childhood. Any attempt to do so, would and could only result in a fake autobiography. Demonstrating her continual mistrust of autobiographies, Sarraute, in both the detailed interview with Weiss and with Cismaru, again maintains that her goal in writing *Enfance* was to recapture certain moments and to render the impressions and sensations that coincided with these moments. Moreover, in the detailed interview with Weiss, she further adds that these moments came from the innocent, unclear periods of childhood:

When I wrote *Childhood*, I stopped at the age of twelve, precisely
because it's still an innocent period in which things are not clear and
in which I tried to recover certain moments, certain impressions and
sensations.[41]

For Sarraute, it is crucial to capture these feelings before they are labeled with adult words because adult words both falsify experience and render it traumatizing. To sum up, although Sarraute dislikes the idea of an autobiography, she does aspire to render certain sensitive moments of her childhood via the use of *tropismes* or "tropisms." It is thanks to these three detailed interviews, important pieces of paratextual information, that the reader is made aware of the author's intentions. Therefore, even though Sarraute maintains that *Enfance* is not a report on her entire life nor even a report on all of her childhood, that it is only a continuation of her research on interior movements, she has, in creating *Enfance*, written a work that can well be considered in the light of the concept of "autobiographical space" as defined in this study. According to this definition, it is possible to evaluate an autobiographical narrative in the more general framework of all the different writing strategies that constitute and/or trace a personality.

Enfance incorporates tropisms, a key element in all of Sarraute's work and an element for which she is well-known. These tropisms are made of interior movements that are found at the borders of our consciousness and are the movements that come before as well as prepare our words and actions. Sarraute describes her research in the following manner:

> Ce que je poursuis dans mes livres, c'est une recherche de mouvements intérieurs qui existent chez tous, chez les noirs et chez les blancs et chez les juifs, et partout. Cette oeuvre est poétique dans ce sens qu'elle cherche à recréer une sensation à un certain niveau de profondeur, et à la faire exister par le langage. ... Je crois que ces "tropismes", ces mouvements intérieurs que je cherche à rendre, sont assez difficiles à saisir, à reconstituer, et à ressentir.[42]

It is this focus on tropisms that is her mark of identification. Sarraute herself said during a detailed interview:

> Ainsi, de livre en livre je cherche ces tropismes, ces mouvements dans des domaines différents – j'essaie d'élargir mon domaine.[43]

Furthermore, in *L'Ère du soupçon*, a series of four essays by Sarraute on the status of the novel, she wrote:

> Mon premier livre [*Tropismes*] contenait en germe tout ce que, dans mes ouvrages suivants, je n'ai cessé de développer. Les tropismes ont continué à être la substance vivante de tous mes livres.[44]

And it is precisely this development of her research on tropisms that allowed Sarraute to distinguish herself from the other *Nouveau Roman* authors, particularly in the early evolutionary period of their novels in the second half of the twentieth century:

> dès le départ, il y avait une différence profonde entre eux et moi. Chez moi, tout était composé de mouvements intérieurs, et eux s'attachaient surtout aux descriptions. On a même fini par les appeler "l'École du regard" - dont je ne pouvais pas faire partie, évidemment.[45]

It is interesting to note that while Sarraute disassociates herself from the other *Nouveau Roman* authors, she does associate herself with Marcel Proust: "Je m'étais un peu inspirée de l'idée que je me faisais du jeune Proust quand on le considérait comme un mondain qui s'occupait de banalités de salon, alors qu'il était en train de chercher une substance inconnue."[46] Indeed, Sarraute has concentrated her efforts on searching for tropisms in common everyday expressions and actions. Raylene O'Callaghan, in her article "The Art of the (Im)Possible: The Autobiography of the French New Novelists," points out an important aspect of Sarraute and Proust's work: the study of the workings of memory, especially affective or involuntary memory.[47]

In *Enfance*, Sarraute succeeds in transmitting impressions of her childhood by means of a unique series of unconnected dialogues which are made up of images and evocative words. These dialogues consist of exchanges among three main voices: one voice belongs to the author-narrator struggling to remember her past; the second represents a sort of alter ego of the first; and the third is that of the young Natacha, the child protagonist of *Enfance*. An autobiography does not normally contain dialogues because this would give a kind of signal of fictionality that would risk being improbable in this context. In contrast, in *Enfance*, the dialogue is related to the present moment of writing, not to the quoting of past voices. As an original creative strategy, these dialogues make *Enfance* an unparalleled example of "writing the self" and are well worth studying for their innovative and complex narrative power.

Also to be kept in mind while analyzing *Enfance* is Michel Beaujour's definition of the self-portrait. According to Beaujour, a self-portrait is a description of the author at the actual time of her/his writing, is written in the present tense, and its main emphasis is on a thematic or logical principle. The self-portrait is not a description of past events, although past events may be described in order to better delineate the present state of the author.[48] His definition could alter one's view of *Enfance*, since *Enfance* appears to be composed solely of loosely connected fragments and lacks a continuous narrative. This impression is further reinforced by Sarraute's focusing on sensations and feelings from her childhood that could serve as the thematic or logical principle of *Enfance*. However, Beaujour's definition of the self-portrait is not aptly applied to *Enfance*, since Sarraute does give an account of what she did as a child and since she does introduce and describe those individuals that surrounded her. Furthermore, *Enfance* is not a portrait of the current situation or circumstances of Sarraute;[49] it is a *retrospective*, although disconnected, autobiographical portrayal of her childhood.

Enfance is a noteworthy text in the study of "writing the self." The first thing that captures the reader's attention is the fact that *Enfance* begins with a dialogue between two voices.[50] It is in effect a text divided into sequences of separate dramatic scenes where the dialogic form constantly interrupts the narrative and is therefore the main means by which the narrative progresses. The dialogues sometimes focus on how one writes and sometimes it corrects, revises, specifies, and continues the narrative.[51] These dramatic scenes, which are concise summaries of particular moments from Sarraute's childhood, are neither numbered nor titled nor have any indication of theme. Since *Enfance* opens in the middle of a discussion between these two voices questioning the whole autobiographical writing process, from the start Sarraute forces the reader to participate more actively in the writing and reading of the text. These voices, by the questions that they raise, establish and maintain the contact between the reader and the text. I would like to point out the difference between my opinion and that of Michael Sheringham on the effect that the device of the two voices has on the role of the reader. While I am of the opinion that it is through the device of the two voices that the reader participates more actively in the writing and reading of the text, Sheringham believes that the reader is excluded from the discussion so that Sarraute is able to shield herself. In his article, *"Ego redux*? Strategies in New French Autobiography,"* he states: "initially it seems quite liberating, to open up the process of autobiography, to involve the reader more. But often it seems to do -- and to be designed to do -- precisely the opposite: to forestall the reader's response, to shut us out of the action, to protect the writer from us."[52] This may very well be the case for many readers since perhaps the reader becomes a listener, overhearing an inner debate. However, the reader is also obliged, finally, to take sides and to make judgements as one certainly becomes aware of the uncertain nature of the autobiographical memory process.

Once accustomed to these two voices, the reader wonders to whom they belong. The reader's first reaction is to suppose that these voices belong to two different characters. Little by little, however, the reader realizes that one voice is that of the author-narrator trying to remember and that the other voice incarnates a sort of alter ego of the first. In fact, the interplay of these two voices constitutes, perhaps paradoxically, a form of interior monologue. In this case, the two voices are both narrators who are combining forces to recount a single story and comment on its production by means of an interior conversation.

The two voices have distinct functions whose differences are revealing. For example, a mediating role is assumed by the voice of the alter ego and at times, the questions posed by this voice anticipate -- in part at least -- the questions that the reader might ask:

> – Alors, tu vas vraiment faire ça? "Évoquer tes souvenirs d'enfance"
> ... Comme ces mots te gênent, tu ne les aimes pas. Mais reconnais
> que ce sont les seuls mots qui conviennent. Tu veux "évoquer tes
> souvenirs" ... il n'y a pas à tortiller, c'est bien ça.[53]

Acting as an intermediary for the reader, the voice of the alter ego thus makes a metacommentary about what is said by the voice of the author-narrator trying to remember and also about what is not said.[54] A result of this metacommentary by the voice of the alter ego is to fill in gaps of information for the reader. These gaps are framed by elliptical marks (...) to show the omission of a clearly implied word or expression. Although the elliptical marks represent blank spaces or small pauses within the narrative, they do not interfere with the continuity of the narrative. They are the means by which the reader is able to perceive how the author-narrator tries to remember, to find the correct expression to properly evoke a childhood memory, and consequently demonstrate obliquely to the reader the problematic nature of autobiography. The discourse of the alter ego, too, is presented with elliptical marks since in its desire to describe the past in accurate detail, like the author-narrator, it will sometimes hesitate over its choice of words. The hesitations by one voice also serve to stimulate the memory process of the other, as in the above cited example, for the response of the voice of the author-narrator trying to remember is: " – Oui, je n'y peux rien, ça me tente, je ne sais pas pourquoi ..." (7) The completion of this dialogic exchange between the two voices shows how they will work together to narrate as precisely as possible memories from the past (the dialogic form of the exchange between ego and alter ego is always set off in the text by a dash, denoting direct discourse):[8]

> – C'est peut-être ... est-ce que ce ne serait pas ... on ne s'en rend parfois pas compte ... c'est peut-être que tes forces déclinent ...
>
> – Non, je ne crois pas ... du moins je ne le sens pas ...
>
> – Et pourtant ce que tu veux faire ... "évoquer tes souvenirs"... est-ce que ce ne serait pas ...
>
> – Oh, je t'en prie ... (7-8)

The voice of the alter ego adds a new dimension to the text by representing the conscious awareness of the process of recollection and the process of writing about it. It often seems to the reader as though the voice of the alter ego is present in order not only to scrutinize and verify what the other voice is recounting, but also to emphasize the retrospective point of view that occurs in the traditional autobiographical writing process. Thus, while the voice of the author-narrator is trying to remember and trying to examine its past, it is being cross-examined by the voice of the alter ego. This adds a broader perspective to the narrative of evoked memories. Sarraute herself recognized that the form of dialogue lead to the emergence of a second voice functioning as a conscience, a voice that was not only the catalyst for *Enfance* but also the controller of what she wrote:

> **JW**: Your most recent book, *Childhood*, is altogether different once again. Why did you use the form of dialogue to recall these memories?
>
> **NS**: That came about naturally, because I told myself, "It's not possible for you to write that." Until that point, I had always written fiction. I had a great freedom, I invented situations in which I placed things that interested me under a certain light. And in *Childhood* I would be bound to something that was fixed, that was already past. It was the opposite of everything I'd done. So I told myself, "You can't do that." I wrote down this dialogue, and it served as the start of my book. After that, all through the book I had this second conscience, which was a double of myself and which controls what I'm doing, which helps me move forward.[55]

Acknowledging the value of the second voice, her "authorial double" in *Enfance*, Sarraute states: "My double is my reasonable side, the one who rereads, the ideal reader that any writer dreams of. I do like Gide: I write in a feat of folly and then I read my text in the frenzy of reason."[56] In this translated comment, the statement, "I do like Gide," refers to the fact that Sarraute's work habits are similar to those of

Gide's. This statement does not refer to whether or not Sarraute likes or dislikes Gide's work.

Yet even though the primary role of the second voice is to serve as a judge and a controller of what the first voice says, there exists an element of collaborative effort between the two voices, even a camaraderie. In regards to this combined effort of the two voices, Lejeune writes:

> De bavarder entre amies. De prendre le relais. De renchérir par d'autres exemples. Ce sont des moments de détente, de récréation. On finirait presque par parler à la fois. On ne sait plus qui est qui: deux soeurs qui se racontent leurs communs souvenirs, et qui parlent en chant amébée.[57]

Nonetheless, unlike Lejeune who refers to the two voices as *deux soeurs* or "two sisters" in order to stress their closeness, some critics are convinced that the two voices are gender-marked.[58] To be able to follow the arguments of these critics, the reader must be extremely attentive in order to distinguish the one example of "gender-marking" of the second voice. The voice of the alter ego could be considered as masculine only at the beginning of *Enfance*, when the voice of the author-narrator trying to remember says that "he," the voice of the alter ego, is grandiloquent and presumptuous (*outrecuidant*): " – Oui, ça te rend grandiloquent. Je dirai même outrecuidant." (8-9) However, knowing that Sarraute is opposed to the idea of gender differences in writing (it is well known that Sarraute refused to attend a conference in the United States when she later discovered that it was billed as a conference on feminist writers) and that *only one example* of gender difference occurs in the entire text, I find it difficult to believe that she wanted to differentiate between the two voices according to their respective genders. Some critics might argue that one of the dialoguing voices is marked as feminine. However, these feminine markings occur only when reference is made to the little girl or to the author. I believe that Sarraute wants the "te" to be neuter, an alter ego without gender. To support my argument, one needs only to read the preface to *L'Ère du soupçon*. In it, Sarraute shows her opposition to gender differences in her work when she writes about the universality of tropisms:

> À ces mouvements qui existent chez tout le monde et peuvent à tout moment se déployer chez n'importe qui, des personnages anonymes, à peine visibles, devaient servir de simple support. [9]

Furthermore, when speaking with Simone Benmussa, Sarraute maintains that her use of the adjective *outrecuidant* in *Enfance* is to be understood as neuter, even though, according to French grammar it could be understood as masculine since it is attributed to a person.[59] What is therefore important to keep in mind is the function of the two voices in the context of *Enfance* and in the context of the reading process. Identification with the child Natacha that arises from subjective feelings or emotions is ascribed to the voice of the author-narrator trying to remember, while the voice of the alter ego is objective, rational, precise, and accurate. The reader can also assume this critical stance as the questions posed by the voice of the alter ego seem to speak for the reader and give the reader the impression of taking part in the discussion. One is encouraged to take sides and make judgments as the uncertain nature of the autobiographical memory process becomes more apparent. For example, the voice of the alter ego interrupts the voice of the author-narrator when it is giving an account of a picture in Natacha's favorite book:

> — Est-il certain que cette image se trouve dans *Max et Moritz*? Ne vaudrait-il pas mieux le vérifier?

> — Non, à quoi bon? Ce qui est certain, c'est que cette image est restée liée à ce livre et qu'est resté intact le sentiment qu'elle me donnait d'une appréhension, d'une peur qui n'était pas de la peur pour de bon, mais juste une peur drôle, pour s'amuser. (48)

Here, the voice of the alter ego wants to verify the exact details of the memory while the voice of the author-narrator concentrates on the feeling that has remained intact even after many years have passed. Another explanation on the dialogic exchange between the two voices has been put forth by Raylene O'Callaghan as she directs our attention to Julia Kristéva's view on the bisexuality of speaking subjects:

> as Julia Kristéva expresses it, all speaking subjects have a certain bisexuality which is precisely the possibility to explore all the sources of signification. This bisexuality is manifest in the two opposing projects, one a narcissistic self-purging of reminiscence, of subtle sensations and suspended states, the other the constitution of knowledge. One reminisces and the other works on the phonetic texture of language, its syntactical articulation of the theoretical conflicts of our time: one posits meaning, the other multiplies, pulverises and finally revives it. Such a bisexuality which does not attempt to expel the other in a power struggle, would seem to characterize the structure of *Enfance* and its two voices eminently well.[60]

Therefore, although the second voice raises queries about what the first voice is trying to remember, it actually serves the important function of complementing or reinforcing the first voice by serving as a stimulus to the memory process.

However, these two voices must be distinguished, as the reader soon begins to realize, from the voice of the child Natacha. When Sarraute does present Natacha's point of view, she uses first-person narration as well as the dramatic present to describe past experiences in order to heighten the intensity of the memory. This use of the present tense is a deviation from the conditions stipulated by Lejeune's pact. According to Lejeune, in a traditional autobiography, the use of the past tense allows for the reader to be able to distinguish between the time of the experience (past tense) and the time of the narration (present tense). Furthermore, according to Paul Ricoeur, to narrate a story is to reflect upon the event narrated. To keep these distinctions in mind, it is helpful to consider the narrative process as divided into *énonciation* and *énoncé*. That is to say, a narrator narrating at the level of *énonciation* will draw attention to the here and now of the present state of the writing process and what the narrator narrates at the level of *énoncé* is the narrative discourse. When distinguishing between *énonciation* and *énoncé*, a two-fold problem occurs. Ricoeur throws light upon this problem:

> Si c'est dans le récit lui-même qu'il faut discerner entre l'énonciation (le discours au sens de Benveniste) et l'énoncé (le récit chez Benveniste), le problème devient alors double: c'est d'une part, celui des rapports entre le temps de l'énonciation et le temps de l'énoncé; d'autre part, celui du rapport entre ces deux temps et le temps de la vie ou de l'action.[61]

Thus, as readers, we must be careful to discern between these two levels. In *Enfance*, these two levels will be used by three distinct first-person voices. For instance, Sarraute presents the point of view of the voice of the child Natacha -- speaking for herself in direct discourse -- in the present tense at the level of *énoncé*. Passages that use the point of view of the voice of the child Natacha are distinguished from passages where the voice of the author-narrator, as if under hypnosis, takes on the point of view of herself as a child. The point of view of the voice of the child Natacha will tend mainly to use direct discourse, whereas the voice of the disembodied author will use present and past tenses. The voice of the author-narrator trying to remember will relate the story in the present tense at the level of *énoncé* but will digress from its narrative discourse to make metacommentaries on the writing and memory process at the level of *énonciation*. It is via the instigation of the voice of the alter ego's probing questions that the voice of the author-narrator trying to remember will deviate from its narrating process at the level of *énoncé* to make a digressive commentary at the level of *énonciation*. Bruno Vercier writes about this technique of Sarraute:

> Interrompant le récit de scansions inattendues, l'autre voix oblige à le compliquer, elle en fait un objet problématique, toujours en mouvement et en transformation. À l'intérieur du fragment que constitue chaque souvenir, elle provoque une fragmentation seconde

qui empêche le récit de "prendre".[62]

There are consequently three well-defined but overlapping first-person narrative voices in *Enfance*. Leah Hewitt, in her book, *Autobiographical Tightropes*, explains (she refers to the voice of the author-narrator trying to remember as the "adult storytelling voice" and the voice of the alter ego as the "adult censuring voice"): "The constitution of the autobiographical subject becomes all the more complex when one realizes that neither of the initiating voices on the first page of *Childhood* is identical to that of the child Nathalie. ... The adult storytelling voice is, in fact, quite close to the child's, and only becomes distinguishable from the latter when the two adult voices appear in dialogue, primarily when the censuring voice doubts an interpretation by the storyteller."[63] To be more precise, the recollection of a past experience in the present tense is at times interrupted by the dialogue between the voice of the author-narrator trying to remember and the voice of the alter ego whose primary function is to clarify the memory process. Especially complex are passages when the voice of the author-narrator takes on -- as if under hypnosis -- the point of view of herself as a child, bringing to the surface a particular experience from the past:

> Comme elle est belle ... je ne peux m'en détacher, je serre plus fort la main de maman, je la retiens pour que nous restions là encore quelques instants, pour que je puisse encore regarder dans la vitrine cette tête ... la contempler ... (91)

However, before the entire experience has been evoked, the voice of the alter ego will interrupt this recollection to ask the voice of the author-narrator to clarify what was so fascinating about the doll's hair:

> — Il est difficile de retrouver ce que cette poupée de coiffeur avait de si fascinant.

> – Je n'y arrive pas bien. Je ne parviens à revoir que son visage assez
> flou, lisse et rose ... lumineux ... comme éclairé au-dedans ... et aussi
> la courbe fière de ses narines, de ses lèvres dont les coins se relèvent
> ... C'est mon émerveillement qui surtout me revient ... tout en elle
> était beau. La beauté, c'était cela. C'était cela - être belle. (91)

As readers we know that the voice of the alter ego is addressing its question to the voice of the author-narrator trying to remember as the words *retrouver* ("to find again") and *revoir* ("to see again") are used. In addition, the voice of the author-narrator gradually slides from the present to the past tense, as she dwells on the recollection from the distant past. There is, then, a switch in narration from the dialogic form back to the voice of the author rendering the point of view of herself as a child in such a way that the reader again has the impression of a disembodied author:

> Je sens soudain comme une gêne, une légère douleur ... on
> dirait que quelque part en moi je me suis cognée contre quelque
> chose, quelque chose est venu me heurter ... ça se dessine, ça prend
> forme ... une forme très nette: "Elle est plus belle que maman." (91-
> 92)

Sarraute, in presenting a detailed account, as if presently relived, of the point of view of the child Natacha reinforces the autobiographer's belief that it is possible to accurately relate memories from the past despite objections to the contrary from the skeptical voice of the alter ego. Then, as the voice of the alter ego continues to explore further the reasons why the young Natacha suddenly felt embarrassed or distressed about considering a doll as more beautiful than her mother, it again engages in dialogue with the voice of the author-narrator:

> – D'où est-ce venu tout à coup?

> – Je me suis longtemps contentée, quand il m'arrivait plus tard de
> repenser à cet instant ...

– Avoue que tu ne l'as pas fait souvent ...

– C'est vrai. Et je ne m'y arrêtais jamais longtemps ... je m'imaginais vaguement que cette importance que j'avais semblé attacher à l'idée de "beauté" avait dû me venir de maman. Qui d'autre qu'elle aurait pu me l'inculquer? Elle avait sur moi un tel pouvoir de suggestion. Elle avait dû m'amener ... sans jamais l'exiger ...elle m'avait sûrement incitée, sans que je sache comment, à la trouver très belle, d'une incomparable beauté ... C'est de là que cela m'était venu, ce malaise, cette gêne ... (92)

Thus, the voice of the author-narrator, and its disembodied counterpart, summoning a view of herself as a child, serve the function of trying to correctly and more completely render childhood memories. In turn, this process is subjected to scrutiny by the voice of the alter ego who is leery of the possibility of verisimilitude in autobiography.

With an understanding of the distinction between the voices in *Enfance*, it is now possible to examine in greater detail the interaction between them. Essentially, the interruptions of the narrative of childhood memories by the voice of the alter ego are metatextual passages since they break the flow of the narrative discourse to make commentaries on what is in the process of being told and how it is being told. The voice of the alter ego will, for example, tease the voice of the author-narrator about the *beaux souvenirs d'enfance* or "beautiful childhood memories" since it is very suspicious of such artificial clichés. It is, in fact, observing closely what is being told and how it is told, carefully scrutinizing both. Furthermore, it is even possible to say that these passages do not form a part of the narrative discourse. Rather they reinforce the function of communication with the reader, anticipating the very questions that the reader would like to ask and thus giving her/him the impression of participating in the interrogation of what the other voice says. This can even give the reader the sense of conducting this interrogation her/himself, albeit at a remove. For example, at the very beginning of *Enfance*, the voice of the alter ego asks the first voice, the voice of the author-narrator, if in evoking her memories, she is not abandoning her domain or field of writing:

> – Si, il faut se le demander: est-ce que ce ne serait pas prendre ta retraite? te ranger? quitter ton élément, où jusqu'ici, tant bien que mal ... (8)

The voice of the alter ego, like a knowledgeable reader, is referring to Sarraute's research on tropisms and to the fact that *Enfance*, as an autobiographical project, would appear to be an abandonment of her usual work. This metatextual passage not only comments on the status of *Enfance* in relation to Sarraute's other work, but anticipates, at least in part, the initial reaction the reader might have to this text itself. The second voice thus fills the important function of foreseeing the reader's reaction and asking the questions that the reader would like to ask.

Another telling example of how the voice of the alter ego anticipates the questions that the reader might ask occurs as part of a dialogue in which the first voice describes what happened one day in Paris when her mother was reading her a story. Even though she can no longer hear the sound of her mother's voice, she still has the impression that, rather than to her, it was to someone else that her mother was telling the story. Then the second voice, that of the alter ego, asks probing questions about the past and consequently serves the function of scrutinizing the process of describing the past:

> – Ne te fâche pas, mais ne crois-tu pas que là, avec ces roucoulements, ces pépiements, tu n'as pas pu t'empêcher de placer un petit morceau de préfabriqué ... c'est si tentant ... tu as fait un joli petit raccord, tout à fait en accord ...
>
> – Oui, je me suis peut-être un peu laissé aller ...
>
> – Bien sûr, comment résister à tant de charme ... à ces jolies sonorités ... roucoulements ...pépiements ... (20-21)

Here, the second voice, by interrupting the narrative discourse, functions to provoke a critical discussion on the choice of language employed by the first voice. In so doing, the second voice points clearly to the problem that arises from the temporal gap between an event and its notation. That is to say, since a long period of time has elapsed since the event took place, it is not unreasonable to assume that the first voice's memory may be faulty. In addition, this critical discussion enables the second voice and the reader to succeed in understanding the relationship between narrative process and reference to actual past experrience because the first voice responds to the second voice by saying:

> — Bon, tu as raison ... mais pour ce qui est des clochettes, des sonnettes, ça non, je les entends ... et aussi des bruits de crécelle, le crépitement des fleurs de celluloïd rouges, roses, mauves, tournant au vent ... (21)

Since language is used as a form of mediation, a distinction must be drawn between what was prefabricated and the present sensation that Sarraute has about this past event and is able to render in such a way that it is as close as possible to the "truth" of the past. The first voice, while admitting that the second is right in this digressive reflection on the choice of vocabulary and descriptive details, justifies what it had narrated by clarifying what was prefabricated and what really existed.

A third example reveals another aspect of the interaction between the two voices while they deliberate over the separation of Natacha from her mother (the second voice speaks first):

> — Il est étrange que ce soit juste cette fois-là que tu aies ressenti pour la première fois une telle détresse au moment de ton départ ... On pourrait croire à un pressentiment ...
>
> — Ou alors chez maman ...
>
> — Oui, quelque chose qui t'aurait fait sentir que cette fois ce n'était pas

un départ comme les autres ...

– J'ai peine à croire, oui, peine, au sens propre du mot, que déjà à ce moment-là elle ait pu envisager ... Non, il n'est pas possible qu'elle ait délibérément voulu me laisser à mon père.

– Ne nous suffit-il pas de constater que nous étions en février et que tu savais que la séparation serait plus longue que d'ordinaire, puisque cette fois, tu devais rester chez ton père plus de deux mois ... jusqu'à la fin de l'été. (108)

This time, the second voice tries to help the first to understand better the feelings of the past associated with the moment of the mother's departure; however, instead of attacking the first voice, as is often the case, the second voice is conciliatory, using rational arguments in order to avoid what might turn into emotional turmoil. The function of this dialogue between the two voices is to focus on an aspect of the lived experience of the past, a separation, and its emotional impact rather than dispute the accuracy of the memory or the choice of language.

Yet, even though the second voice's primary role is to carefully listen to and observe what the first voice recounts and to help the first voice to go as far as possible in its analyses, the second voice often pushes the first voice to the point of exasperation, so that the first voice becomes indignant and either takes charge of the narrative situation or challenges in turn the second voice. For example, when asking for more precise details about the young Natacha's outings with the maid whose hair is saturated with vinegar, the second voice asks: "– Pour faire quoi?"(23) The first voice, obviously irritated by this question, responds in a very agitated manner:

– Ah, n'essaie pas de me tendre un piège ... Pour faire n'importe quoi, ce que font tous les enfants qui jouent, courent, poussent leurs bateaux, leurs cerceaux, sautent à la corde, s'arrêtent soudain et l'oeil fixe observent les autres enfants, les gens assis sur les bancs de pierre, sur les chaises ... ils restent plantés devant eux bouche bée... (23-24)

However, the second voice persists: "– Peut-être le faisais-tu plus que d'autres, peut-être autrement ..." (24) To which the first voice replies even more insistently:

> – Non, je ne dirai pas ça ... je le faisais comme le font beaucoup d'enfants ... et avec probablement des contestations et des réflexions du même ordre ... en tout cas rien ne m'en est resté et ce n'est tout de même pas toi, qui vas me pousser à chercher à combler ce trou par un replâtrage. (24)

The function of this exchange between the two voices is ideological in that the first voice refuses to narrate what has disappeared from memory. Digressing somewhat uncharacteristically from the story it is telling, the first voice defends the fragmentary nature of past memories that impedes the precision that an autobiographer strives to achieve in recollection and the ensuing writing process.

The first voice is also capable of taking a strong stance in the face of the attack of the second voice's questions. A heated interaction between the two voices serves the function of showing the reader how the autobiographer does attempt to investigate fully the past, and it is through the dialogic exchange between the two voices that the most intricate feelings and details emerge from the past. As an example of the first voice refuting one of the second voice's questions, one needs only to examine the first voice's reaction when the two are discussing the warmth of the relationship between Natacha's "real mother"[64] and her second husband Kolia (the second voice speaks first):

> – Une fois pourtant ... tu te rappelles ...

> – Mais c'est ce que j'ai senti longtemps après ... tu sais bien que sur le moment ... (73-74)

The second voice, in constantly interrogating the first voice, forces it not only to become defensive and more accurate in its details, but eventually, through this coaxing, the first voice begins to anticipate the second voice's questions before they have been asked. Consequently, the first voice becomes more rational and less emotional in its thinking. For example, when reflecting upon the ensuing separation from the real mother, the first voice becomes aware of the limitations of its memory without the intervention of the second voice:

> Je suis assise au bord de mon lit, le dos tourné à la fenêtre, je tiens debout sur mes genoux mon compagnon, mon confident, mon ours en pelage doré, tout mou et doux, et je lui raconte ce que maman vient de me dire ... "Tu sais, nous allons bientôt revenir à Paris, chez papa ... plus tôt que d'habitude ... et là-bas, figure-toi qu'il y aura une autre maman ..."
> Alors maman qui est là, qui m'entend, me dit d'un air fâché: "Mais qu'est-ce que tu racontes? Quelle autre maman? on ne peut pas en avoir une autre. Tu n'as au monde qu'une seule maman." *Je ne sais si elle a prononcé ces phrases ou seulement la dernière d'entre elles*, mais j'y retrouve l'emphase inhabituelle avec laquelle elle m'a parlé, et qui m'a rendue muette, comme pétrifiée. (104, my italics)

In this example, Sarraute uses the voice of the disembodied author-narrator to begin the story. The story is then interrupted by the direct discourse of the voice of the child Natacha. The use of direct discourse allows for the focus to be on the spoken so that directly quoted (or actually pronounced) phrases from the past are reproduced on the level of the narrative. In addition, the use of direct discourse gives the impression of immediacy and accuracy. In this example, the third voice not only relates its own words but directly quotes the words of the mother as well. When the spoken discourse of the third voice is complete, the first voice takes over to reflect on the memory process. It is apparent that the first voice takes over the telling of the story for, beginning with "Je ne sais si elle a prononcé ces phrases," the past tense is used to signal the metacommentary on the memory process made at the level of *énonciation*.[65] In this passage, we see that in recalling the story, the first voice is capable of recognizing the limitations of its memory without the interference of the second voice. This is in sharp contrast to other moments when this recognition is dependent on aggressive questioning.

Nonetheless, the role of the second voice is not simply to serve as an antagonizing stimulus to the first voice. The reader will also note that at times, as here, there is a bonding process between the voices. There are scenes where the second voice becomess melancholic and identifies with the first voice as they discuss a past memory. For example, when discussing the stepmother Véra's passionate love for her daughter Lili, it is the second voice that reminisces and comments as it expresses an understanding that had neither been fully registered in the mind of the child Natacha at the time of the incident, nor had been manifested in the text by the voice of author-narrator trying to remember:

> – Une passion unique. Lili était sa maladie. Et cette fureur, on sentait qu'elle n'était pas vraiment dirigée contre Lili, mais contre quelque chose qui était au-delà d'elle ...c'est sur cela que Véra fixait ce regard obstiné, implacable ... sur un destin qu'elle voulait vaincre à tout prix ... elle compenserait, elle ferait plus encore que compenser tout ce qu'il refuserait à son enfant, elle le transformerait coûte que
>
> coûte pour en faire le meilleur, le plus enviable destin du monde. (145)

In this dialogic probing, past actions and feelings are analyzed and interpreted. In addition, there is a definite congruence of purpose between the two voices in this instance, as it is the second voice that contemplates and reflects on the memory and provides the details while the first voice listens. Thus, the forces of the two voices merge in a single effort to not simply reproduce or recall past actions, but to analyze them in the flow of the writing so as to search out their significance. Vercier astutely explains this function of the two voices:

> Par le dialogue de ses deux voix, Nathalie Sarraute apporte également une solution globale qui se pose à tout autobiographe: écrire au

> présent une histoire passée, c'est-à-dire non pas reproduire des comportements, mais les analyser dans le mouvement de l'écriture, en chercher la signification.[66]

Furthermore, this collaborative effort on the part of the two voices to discover the significance of past actions is important to the reading process. The reader's involvement with the text is enhanced since one has the impression of being able to observe firsthand the struggles of the autobiographer as she attempts to recount her past. As Valerie Minogue points out: "The reader is kept aware of the doubts and challenges that arise in the act of narration. We are not plunged into a childhood, we are plunged into the process of remembering and writing it, a process acknowledged as partial, selective and interpretative."[67] Thus, by using the technique of two voices dialoguing in the present tense, Sarraute invites her readers to participate in her autobiographical writing process. This technique also enables her to search for the diverse hidden meanings of a past event and to show the memory's imperfections while in the midst of the writing process. But it also allows the reader to have more confidence in the narrative truth value of *Enfance*, since the "memories" of the first voice are continually scrutinized and challenged by the second.

However, these questioning and controlling measures by the second voice, which all contribute in forcing the first voice to be as honest and as exact as possible in its remembering process, do not prevent the first voice from preserving and transmitting to the reader the sensation of the evoked memory. For example, when discussing the aftereffects of Natacha's attempt to steal a sachet of sugared almonds because Véra had refused to buy her one, the second voice's questions push the first voice to explore further the memory process. The result is that the first voice not only renders the feelings of guilt associated with the incident but the father's suffering as well:

> – Ces paroles le rendent furieux ... Il les répète: "Parce que j'en avais envie! J'en avais envie! Alors je me permets n'importe quoi! Je me

fais prendre comme une voleuse, je fais du mal aux autres ... J'en ai
envie, eh bien, je fais tout ce qui me passe par la tête ... Voyez-vous
ça, j'en ai envie ... il me semble que maintenant il souffre et rage pour
de bon ... Mais moi, est-ce que tu t'imagines que je fais tout ce dont
j'ai envie? Mais qu'est-ce que tu crois? ... J'en ai tellement envie,
alors plus rien ne me retient, plus rien ne compte..." Ces paroles
furibondes me traversent et vont quelque part ailleurs, au-delà de moi
..." Ah, quand on a une nature comme celle-là ... je sens maintenant
sur moi son dégoût ... je peux même le dire, je n'exagère pas ... sa
haine ... Alors je me tourne vers le mur ... Il dit encore quelques mots
comme ... Ce sera joli plus tard, ça promet, ça donnera de beaux
résultats ..." et il sort en refermant rageusement la porte. (157-158)

The ability of this passage to successfully transmit to the reader the sensation of the
evoked memory comes essentially from the use of direct discourse, the exchange
between Natacha and her father, in particular the ironic repetition of the words "J'en
avais envie!"

To analyze fully the use of direct discourse by the voices in *Enfance*, one
must examine the bond between childhood memories and memories of particular
word phrases from Sarraute's childhood. The word phrases from the past, reproduced
directly in the narrative discourse, evoke childhood memories because they are word
phrases that have lingered in Sarraute's memory. The reason that certain words had
a profound impression and the reason that she was successful in reproducing these
impressions in *Enfance* stems from the fact that they originated from a situation in
which Natacha was emotionally hurt or wounded, or these words might have been
the cause of the emotional wound.[68] The word phrases evoke simple images or have
a haunting quality and may appeal to similar memories of the reader. To illustrate
this aspect of images in Sarraute's work, consider closely the scene where Natacha
finds herself in the dining room of a Swiss hotel where children take their meals
under the watchful eye of their maids and governesses. This scene highlights
perfectly her suffering through the recall of word phrases associated with one parent,
accentuating the fact that she is constantly being pulled in two directions by spending
time alternately with her father and her mother. In this scene, Natacha is conscious

of the abusive words of the adults even though she is separated from the other children:

> "Allons, avale, arrête ce jeu idiot, ne regarde pas cet enfant, tu ne dois pas l'imiter, c'est un enfant insupportable, c'est un enfant fou, un enfant maniaque ..." (14)

But nothing will convince Natacha to eat more quickly because before her departure to meet with her father, her mother had insisted on this promise:

> "Tu as entendu ce qu'a dit le docteur Kervilly? Tu dois mâcher les aliments jusqu'à ce qu'ils deviennent aussi liquides qu'une soupe ... Surtout ne l'oublie pas, quand tu seras là-bas, sans moi, là-bas on ne saura pas, là-bas on oubliera, on n'y fera pas attention, ce sera à toi d'y penser, tu dois te rappeler ce que je te recommande ... promets-moi que tu le feras ... – Oui, je te le promets, maman, sois tranquille, ne t'inquiète pas, tu peux compter sur moi..." (15-16)

It is at that moment that the words "aussi liquide qu'une soupe" were engraved in her memory, and make her realize that she alone has the responsibility for her own behavior in the mother's absence. It is important to remind ourselves that Sarraute insists upon the fact that even though these exact words and images could not have been formed either in the head of a child or of an adult, it is these words and images that help to seize and retain the sensations from the past. Once again, she employs the technique of two voices (the second voice interrogates):

> – Des images, des mots qui évidemment ne pouvaient pas se former à cet âge-là dans ta tête ...

> – Bien sûr que non. Pas plus d'ailleurs qu'ils n'auraient pu se former dans la tête d'un adulte ... C'était ressenti, comme toujours, hors des mots, globalement ... Mais ces mots et ces images sont ce qui permet de saisir tant bien que mal, de retenir ces sensations. (17)

These words, "aussi liquide au'une soupe," locked up within her, give her the courage to persist, backed up, as it were, by the partial presence of the mother through this refrain:

> Je supporte vaillamment les blâmes, les moqueries, l'exclusion, les accusations de méchanceté, l'inquiétude qui produit ici ma folie, le sentiment de culpabilité ... mais qu'a-t-il de comparable avec celui que j'éprouverais si, reniant ma promesse, bafouant des paroles devenues sacrées, perdant tout sens du devoir, de la responsabilité, me conduisant comme un faible petit enfant je consentais à avaler ce morceau avant qu'il soit devenu "aussi liquide qu'une soupe". (18)

It is also essential to note the severe order, "Nein, das tust du nicht" ("Non, tu ne feras pas ça") [10] that was the opening scene of the autobiographical memory process in *Enfance*. Sarraute even inscribes in the text the potency of these words as she explains via the first voice that they penetrate her today as they did when they were first expressed:

> ... les voici de nouveau, ces paroles, elles se sont ranimées, aussi vivantes, aussi actives qu'à ce moment, il y a si longtemps, où elles ont pénétré en moi, elles appuient, elles pèsent de toute leur puissance, de tout leur énorme poids. (10)

In addition, the words "Nein, das tust du nicht" and Natacha's retaliatory expression 'Ich werde es zerreissen' ("Je vais le déchirer") are particularly noteworthy as they are in German and not in French. After the second voice asks the first voice how she could have learned German so well as a young child, the first voice explains:

> – Oui, je me le demande ... Mais ces paroles, je ne les ai jamais prononcées depuis ... "Ich werde es zerreissen" ... "Je vais le déchirer" ... le mot "zerreissen" rend un son sifflant, féroce, dans une seconde quelque chose va se produire ... je vais déchirer, saccager, détruire ...ce sera une atteinte ... un attentat ... criminel ... mais pas sanctionné comme il pourrait l'être, je sais qu'il n'y aura aucune punition ... (11)

Thus, the repetitive hissing sound of "zerreissen" triggered the recall of the German words of her youth and the scene where, in a hotel room in either Interlaken or Beatenberg, Switzerland, the young woman engaged to look after Natacha and to teach her German, is trying to prevent her from destroying the back of the silk settee with steel scissors.

Word phrases, like "Quel malheur quand même de ne pas avoir de mère." (121), may also be linked to central moments of recognition and as such, may have a devastating effect on the child Natacha. These words were spoken by the woman who had moved Natacha's belongings from her vast bedroom looking out onto the street to a small bedroom by the kitchen. This move was made to accomodate Véra's new baby and the baby's nurse and it was done without consideration for Natacha's feelings. However, the brutality of the action was only fully realized by the child Natacha after the woman's comment. The voice of the disembodied author-narrator explains:

> "Quel malheur!" ... le mot frappe, c'est bien le cas de le dire, de plein fouet. Des lanières qui s'enroulent autour de moi, m'enserrent ... Alors c'est ça, cette chose terrible, la plus terrible qui soit, qui se révélait au-dehors par des visages bouffis de larmes, des voiles noirs, des gémissements de désespoir ... le "malheur" qui ne m'avait jamais approchée, jamais effleurée, s'est abattu sur moi. Cette femme le voit. Je suis dedans. Dans le malheur. Comme tous ceux qui n'ont pas de mère. Je n'en ai donc pas. C'est évident, je n'ai pas de mère. Mais comment est-ce possible? Comment ça a-t-il pu m'arriver, à moi? Ce qui avait fait couler mes larmes que maman effaçait d'un geste calme, en disant: "Il ne faut pas ..." aurait-elle pu le dire si ç'avait été le "malheur"? (121)

Thus, for the first time, Natacha feels trapped in a word. The second voice questions the first voice about this feeling of entrapment: "– C'était la première fois que tu avais été prise ainsi, dans un mot." (122) And the first voice responds:

– Je ne me souviens pas que cela me soit arrivé avant. Mais combien de fois depuis ne me suis-je pas évadée terrifiée hors des mots qui s'abattent sur vous et vous enferment. (122)

In addition, the words "Quel malheur quand même de ne pas avoir de mère" are particularly forceful since the reader feels the damage caused by these words. This is because Sarraute repeatedly portrays Natacha's anguish, since her love for both of her parents is severely tested by their divorce. Phrases such as "aussi liquide qu'une soupe," "Nein, das tust du nicht," "Ich werde es zerreissen," and "Quel malheur quand même de ne pas avoir de mère" may resonate in the reader's memory and trigger a recall of a similar experience.[69]

Word phrases that use figurative language to put into concrete form abstract notions, such as emotions, are particularly forceful in Sarraute's texts.[70] For example, when discussing the aftereffects of having considered a doll as more beautiful than her real mother, the first voice reflects upon the strength of "ideas":

> Je ne crois pas que j'aie jamais été plus seule avant cela - ni même après. Aucune aide à attendre de personne ... Livrée sans défense aux "idées". Un terrain propice sur lequel *elles pouvaient faire tout ce qu'elles voulaient, elles s'ébattaient, s'appelaient entre elles et il en venaient toujours d'autres* ... toutes étaient la preuve indubitable que je n'étais pas un enfant qui aime sa mère. Pas comme doit être un enfant. (100, my italics)

In this example, "ideas" become personified and are invested with animate qualities. In this manner, the first voice continues by telling how "her ideas" came to dominate her childhood:

> Je ne me souviens plus de toutes les idées folles, saugrenues qui sont venues m'habiter ... seulement de la dernière, elle a fort heureusement précédé de peu mon départ, ma séparation d'avec ma mère, qui a mis fin brutalement à ce qui en se développant risquait de devenir une véritable folie. (101)

This "last idea" concerned the mother's stingy allotment of food for the maids. Out of love and devotion for her real mother, the child Natacha fought desperately against this "last idea." However, she fails to conquer it:

> Mais voici qu'à un autre repas, l'idée revient, elle rôde, elle guette ... j'ai peur ... j'essaie de l'empêcher d'entrer, je détourne les yeux, mais quelque chose me pousse, il faut que je voie ... C'est vers le bout du rôti, vers ce morceau plus petit, et cet autre à côté, c'est vers eux que maman avance la fourchette, c'est eux qu'elle pique, soulève et dépose dans l'assiette que lui tend Gacha ... je ne regarde pas le visage de Gacha ... même s'il n'y a pas sur lui l'ombre d'un petit sourire, je sais ce qu'elle pense ... je le pense comme elle. *Mais moi l'idée me déchire, me dévore ... quand elle me lâche, c'est pour un temps, elle va revenir, elle est toujours là, à l'affût, prête à bondir au cours de n'importe quel repas.* (102-103, my italics)

This repeated and extended personification of "ideas" has the effect of intensifying and dramatizing for the reader the anxieties of the young Natacha. The "ideas" are thus not simply described but cast as active forces and brought to life.

A final characteristic of Sarraute's style that is particularly striking in *Enfance* are the sensations that she transmits to the reader via the images that she creates. Once more, I would like to emphasize that the ability to transmit these fleeting sensations or tropisms via words is Sarraute's principal goal. In *L'Ère du soupçon*, she discusses the power of words in helping to transmit sensations or tropisms:

> Mais, à défaut d'actes, nous avons à notre disposition les paroles. Les paroles possèdent les qualités nécessaires pour capter, protéger et porter au-dehors ces mouvements souterrains à la fois impatients et craintifs. (121)

In addition, she commented on the importance of creating simple images in the detailed interview with Finch and Kelley:

> Je prends des images assez simples parce qu'il faut aller vite. Le

lecteur et moi, nous n'avons pas le temps de nous arrêter pour chercher ce que ça veut dire. On sent tout de suite ce que c'est que d'être devant un boa. Il faut que ce soit une image qui se trans-mette tout de suite.[71]

The feeling of being in front of a boa constrictor is one of apprehension and fright. In *Enfance*, Sarraute creates similar sensations. For example, the voice of the child Natacha relates what the real mother had told her when they were walking in the country with Kolia and suddenly found themselves in front of a wooden telegraph pole: "Si tu le touches, tu meurs."(27-28) While reading this passage, I soon became distressed and I shared the feelings of the young Natacha. My anxiety was brought about by Sarraute's narrative strategies that emphasize the fear of the young Natacha. I was very relieved to learn that she had not been injured. In order to understand better my particular reaction as a reader to this passage, it is necessary to examine it in greater detail. The passage reads as follows:

> J'ai envie de le toucher, je veux savoir, j'ai très peur, je veux voir comment ce sera, j'étends ma main, je touche avec mon doigt le bois du poteau électrique ... et aussitôt ça y est, ça m'est arrivé, maman le savait, maman sait tout, c'est sûr, je suis morte, je cours derrière eux en hurlant, je cache ma tête dans les jupes de maman, je crie de toutes mes forces: je suis morte ... ils ne le savent pas, je suis morte ... Mais qu'est-ce que tu as? Je suis morte, morte, morte, j'ai touché le poteau, voilà, ça y est, la chose horrible, la plus horrible qui soit était dans ce poteau, je l'ai touché et elle est passée en moi, elle est en moi, je me roule par terre pour qu'elle sorte, je sanglotte, je hurle, je suis morte ... ils me soulèvent dans leurs bras, ils me secouent, m'embrassent ... Mais non, mais tu n'as rien ... J'ai touché le poteau, maman l'a dit ... elle rit, ils rient tous deux et cela m'apaise ... (28)

There are three noteworthy points concerning this passage that have a special effect on the reader. First, the use of the present tense, creating an illusion of immediacy, gives the reader the impression of being in front of the wooden telegraph pole with the young Natacha; second, the linking of a string of several short jerky phrases stresses the force of the sensations associated with this situation; and third, the use of the elliptical marks here show the intense emotion with which the voice of the disembodied author-narrator is recounting the story as passion speaks more quickly than words can follow it.

In the detailed interview with Besser, Sarraute points out a second important element of her images:

> ... j'emploie des images faciles et claires qui renvoient à des sensations que le lecteur a conscience d'avoir lui-même éprouvées. Par analogie, j'espère qu'il peut retrouver ce que je veux lui montrer.[72]

Empathy based on analogical or similar experiences is a powerful force in Sarraute's narrative. For example, in *Enfance*, there is an image which among all the others remains engraved in my memory and to which I had a very strong reaction because I myself had experienced a similar pain. It is necessary to cite the passage in full in order to illustrate clearly my reaction to Sarraute's style (the voice of the disembodied author-narrator speaks first):

> En entrant dans ma chambre, avant même de déposer mon cartable, je vois que mon ours Michka que j'ai laissé couché sur mon lit ... il est plus mou et doux qu'il n'a jamais été, quand il fait froid je le couvre jusqu'au cou avec un carré de laine tricotée et on n'aperçoit que sa petite tête jaune et soyeuse, ses oreilles amollies, les fils noirs usés de sa truffe, ses yeux brillants toujours aussi vifs ... il n'est plus là ... mais où est-il? Je me précipite ... "Adèle, mon ours a disparu – C'est Lili qui l'a pris ... – Mais comment est-ce possible? – Elle a réussi à marcher jusqu'à ta chambre ... la porte était ouverte... – Où est-il? Où l'a-t-elle mis? – Ah elle l'a déchiré ... ce n'était pas difficile, il ne tenait qu'à un cheveu, ce n'était plus qu'une loque ... – Mais on peut le réparer ... – Non, il n'y a rien à faire, je l'ai jeté ..."
>
> Je ne veux pas le revoir. Je ne dois pas dire un mot de plus sinon Adèle, c'est sûr, va me répondre: Des ours comme ça, on en trouve tant qu'on veut, et des tout neufs, des bien plus beaux ... Je cours dans ma chambre, je me jette sur mon lit, je me vide de larmes

...

– Jamais il ne t'est arrivé d'en vouloir à quelqu'un comme à ce moment-là tu en as voulu à Lili.

– Après j'ai mis hors de sa portée les boîtes russes en bois gravé, la ronde et la rectangulaire, le bol en bois peint, je ne sais plus quels autres trésors, mes trésors à moi, personne d'autre que moi ne connaît leur valeur, il ne faut pas que vienne les toucher, que puisse s'en emparer ce petit être criard, hagard, insensible, malfaisant, ce diable, ce démon ... (185-186)

The dramatic effect of this passage comes from the fact that in two previous passages, Sarraute had described the importance of Michka for the young Natacha.[73] For a young child, torn between the devotion for her two divorced parents, Michka was the only one who was really close to her. In addition, in this passage, Sarraute creates anew, via a switch to directly quoted phrases by the voice of the child Natacha, the scene describing the interaction between Adèle and the young Natacha. That is to say, this use of direct discourse allows for the verbatim rendering of the discussion between Natacha and Adèle. Only at the end of the description of this discussion by the voice of the child Natacha, is there a brief commentary by the voice of the alter ego. Sarraute is thus able to directly reveal to us the young Natacha's feelings and emotions during her agitated reaction to Adèle's explanation. The climactic conclusion of the scene is completed by the voice of the author-narrator trying to remember as it answers the voice of the alter ego's commentary by recounting what happened after this terrible incident: she placed all her valuables out of Lili's reach. Thanks to the dramatic effect of the passage, the use of direct discourse, which brings about the revelation of the young Natacha's feelings, and the mentioning of the aftereffects of the trauma, the reader is fully engaged in the narrative.

In conclusion, going against her long-standing principle that all autobiographies are fake, Nathalie Sarraute in producing *Enfance*, a very selective and partial autobiographical project, not only continues her research on interior movements, but also gives us an innovative example of "writing the self." She achieves this by combining tropisms that transmit the interior movements with voices of the author-narrator who tries to remember, of the author-narrator's alter ego, and of the child Natacha. Throughout the entire text, the dialoguing voices interrupt most of the narrative accounts of scenes from the past, giving the impression of an interior conversation. In such a manner, Sarraute's struggles with the autobiographical writing process are exemplified by the disputes between the voice of the author-narrator and that of its alter ego. The voice of the author-narrator's alter ego serves as Sarraute's questioning self that does not believe in autobiographies, liberating her so she can capture "childhood" sensations before they disappear. Furthermore, her manipulation of the present tense and direct discourse while describing the past gives the reader the impression of being present at the past experience instead of simply being a witness to its depiction. The illusion is strongest in the passages where the voice of the author-narrator trying to remember suddenly switches, as if transfigured, to the child's point of view. This creates a "work in movement," going beyond the fixed, stable, retrospective mode of the conventional autiobiography. How far beyond conventional autobiography is perhaps most dramatically embodied in the metacommentaries (the voice of the author-narrator digresses from the story it is telling at the level of *énoncé* to make metacommentaries on its autobiographical writing process at the level of *énonciation*), which share with the reader the problematic nature of the genre itself. This method is very effective because it makes the reader particularly sensitive to the impressions that Sarraute wants to communicate, while at the same time it gives the author the possibility of searching for the significance of related events. The style of Sarraute is unique from the point of view that she communicates to us remembered sensations via dialogues, images of visions and abstract notions, and evocative words. In *Enfance*, Sarraute presents us with new ways of looking at the world, the self, and the literary text by forcing us to question conventional boundaries.

Nathalie Sarraute died in Paris on October 19, 1999. She was 99 years old and was survived by her three daughters, Claude, Anne, and Dominque. *Enfance* was adapted as a one-act play and presented in New York City with Glenn Close in 1985. Sarraute actively wrote until her death (at home or in her favorite café, the *Trocadéro*, near her home in the 16th arrondissement) and at the time of her death, she was hard at work on yet another book. Her last publications, after *Tu ne t'aimes pas* (1989), were *Ici* (1995) and *Ouvrez* (1997). In 1997, her complete works (seventeen books, including ten novels) were reissued in France's legendary Pléïade series.

Chapter Three

Marguerite Duras' *L'Amant* and Other

"Autofictional Narratives"

M. Duras n'avoue pas, elle (s')
invente. ... Elle ne dit même pas:
voilà ce que je fus, ce que je suis. Elle
dit: voilà ce que je fis, ce que je
vécus, et tout simplement ce qui eut
lieu – c'est-à-dire ce que je peux en
dire aujourd'hui. - Marcelle Marini,
"Une femme sans aveu"[74]

In 1984, *L'Amant*, by Marguerite Duras, won the Prix Goncourt and became

an international best-seller. It has been translated into forty-three languages. Carlin

Romano, of the *Philadelphia Inquirer*, reports that in France alone, *L'Amant* sold

nearly 800,000 copies and led the French best-seller list for six months. He also

gives an account of its publication in the United States: "Two years ago, it was

Umberto Eco's lengthy *The Name of the Rose*, defying the publishing rule that

translations of serious foreign novels can't make the best-seller list. This summer,

it's Marguerite Duras' *The Lover* (...) Published here this summer, it has taken off in

a similar way [as it did in France] going onto national best-seller lists and attracting

enough interest in paperback rights to require an auction (Harper & Row won the

52

bidding this week with an offer of $155,000)."[75]

    L'Amant is an autobiographical work that tells of Duras' childhood in colonial French Indochina - a theme which has appeared and reappeared in many of her "autofictional narratives," most notably in *Un Barrage contre le Pacifique* (1950), *Des Journées entières dans les arbres* (1954), *L'Eden cinéma* (1988), and most recently in *L'Amant de la Chine du nord* (1991). Yet unlike these narratives, where a female character is the subject of third-person narration, in *L'Amant* we can distinguish alternating narrative voices. Among them are the first-person authorial voice of Duras remembering her adolescence and two seemingly distinct omniscient third-person narrators, one offering a second perspective on Duras' adolescence and the other confined to telling about the older Duras. The use of the first-person narration by the author-identified narrator remembering her adolescence, enables Duras to present an omniscient narrator who, with great flexibility, is capable of shifting from one period to another, from one place to another. In addition, the differences between the first- and third-person narrative voices enhance the contrast between internal and external focus. Internal focus permits the unveiling of a character's thoughts and feelings whereas external focus limits the reader to an exterior view of a character or scene. Thus, a narration with an internal focus gives the reader the impression of being more intimately involved with the text. Leah Hewitt speaks of this fascinating technique of Duras' in her book *Autobiographical Tightropes*: "The first-person female (and author-identified) narrative is not, in fact, characteristic of most of the narratives published before *The Lover*. ... This is in part why *The Lover*, as an autobiographical project, is so intriguing: the female narrating voice posits the possibility of resuscitating (creating) her past from her 'own' point of view."[76] Or, as Carol Murphy highlights in her article, "Duras' *L'Amant*: Memories from an Absent Photo," "*L'Amant* is yet another example of this *déformation textuelle* in which Marguerite Duras substitutes herself (the *je* of autobiography) for the fictional narrators in her novels, plays and films. In effect,

Duras fictionalizes her own autobiography."[77] The alternation between the first- and third-person narrations in one text is a key writing strategy employed by Duras in composing the history of her personality. This strategy is of primary importance to this study of Duras works since it helps to resolve part of the difficulty of categorizing *L'Amant*, especially in relation to her other "autofictional narratives," and consequently emphasizes the need to expand Lejeune's notion of "autobiographical space."

It was not until the publication of *L'Amant* that the autobiographical aspects of Duras' previous works became truly evident. In using the first-person narration to relate her adolescence in colonial French Indochina, she finally signed the "autobiographical pact" as defined by Lejeune. That is to say, in *L'Amant* there is an identity among the author, the narrator, and the protagonist or main character. To be kept in mind when examining Duras' strategy of alternating between first- and third-person narrations is Cohn's aforementioned position on the change in narrative climate as one moves between third-person narration and autobiographical first-person narration: "... The narration of inner events is far more strongly affected by this change of person than the narration of outer events; past thought must now be presented as remembered by the self, as well as expressed by the self ..."[78]

To understand more fully Duras' use of three types of narration in *L'Amant*, each type will now be examined. The first type, that of the first-person narration by Duras, the author-identified narrator, remembering her adolescence, is the most prominent. For example, at the very beginning of *L'Amant*, Duras writes:

> Un jour, j'étais âgée déjà, dans le hall d'un lieu public, un homme est venu vers moi. Il s'est fait connaître et il m'a dit: "Je vous connais depuis toujours. Tout le monde dit que vous étiez belle lorsque vous étiez jeune, je suis venu pour vous dire que pour moi je vous trouve plus belle maintenant que lorsque vous étiez jeune, j'aimais moins votre visage de jeune femme que celui que vous avez maintenant, dévasté."[79]

Starting at an undetermined period of time in her recent past where she contemplates her now-ravaged looks, Duras sets the stage for her first-person narration of her adolescence as she draws a parallel to the sooner-than-expected ageing of her younger self. Even though this study does focus primarily on the juxtaposition of first- and third-person narrations, one should note the interweaving of verb tenses and different time periods that are incorporated into the narration of *L'Amant*. This interweaving of verb tenses and different time periods is important since *L'Amant* does not follow a specific chronological order as would a traditional autobiography.

Moreover, in addition to *L'Amant*'s non-chronological narrative, there is a distinction to be made in Duras' writing, as is the case with Sarraute's writing, between narration at the level of *énoncé* and digressive metacommentaries on the autobiographical writing process made at the level of *énonciation*:

> Très vite dans ma vie il a été trop tard. À dix-huit ans il était
> déjà trop tard. Entre dix-huit ans et vingt-cinq ans mon visage est
> parti dans une direction imprévue. À dix-huit ans j'ai vieilli. (9-10)

Here Duras begins the gradual process of recovering her past. She does not begin the narrative of her adolescence at the point at which she met her Northern Chinese lover,[80] but at a point where she has aged, presumably shortly after her affair with him. This technique slowly leads the reader back into Duras' past and shows the multiplicity of time levels in the narration. It is not until one page later when Duras writes the following that she begins the narration of her youth:

> J'ai quinze ans et demi, il n'y a pas de saisons dans ce pays-là,
> nous sommes dans une saison unique, chaude, monotone, nous
> sommes dans la longue zone chaude de la terre, pas de printemps, pas
> de renouveau.
>
> Je suis dans une pension d'État à Saigon. Je dors et je mange là, dans
> cette pension, mais je vais en classe au-dehors, au lycée français. Ma
> mère, institutrice, veut le secondaire pour sa petite fille. (11)

In this example, Duras starts the narration of her youth in the present tense at the level of *énoncé*. It thus sets the stage for the narration's development as she will switch back and forth between verb tenses and time periods, and between first- and third-person narrations. In close proximity to this first-person narration is the first-person commentary on the feasibility of writing her life story:

> L'histoire de ma vie n'existe pas. Ça n'existe pas. Il n'y a jamais de centre. Pas de chemin, pas de ligne. Il y a de vastes endroits où l'on fait croire qu'il y avait quelqu'un, ce n'est pas vrai il n'y avait personne. (14)

In this metacommentary, made at the level of *énonciation*, Duras, commenting on her autobiographical project, exploits the possibilities of first-person narrative, and focusing on the narrator and the situation of narration, remarks on the kinds of narrations she has produced. She continues by differentiating between what she has already written about her youth and the project which she is now undertaking:

> L'histoire d'une toute petite partie de ma jeunesse je l'ai plus ou moins écrite déjà, enfin je veux dire, de quoi l'apercevoir, je parle de celle-ci justement, de celle de la traversée du fleuve. Ce que je fais ici est différent, et pareil. Avant, j'ai parlé des périodes claires, de celles qui étaient éclairées. Ici je parle des périodes cachées de cette même jeunesse, de certains enfouissements que j'aurais opérés sur certains faits, sur certains sentiments, sur certains événements. (14)

Duras thus discriminates here between the clear periods of her youth, which she has already written about in her "autofictional narratives," and the buried facts, feelings, and events which she will now try to reveal in *L'Amant*. Therefore, in making this comment, narrated at the level of *énonciation* with an internal perspective, Duras alludes directly to the autobiographical aspects of her previous writings.

In contrast to the author-identified narrator remembering her adolescence, the two types of third-person narration, that of the third-person narration of Duras' adolescence as seen by the omniscient narrator and that of the third-person narration of the older Duras as seen by the omniscient narrator, are significant in *L'Amant* as they provide Duras with the means of designating her alter ego by the indefinite "she." This technique also allows her to distance herself from her text without, on the other hand, letting fiction go free. She is able to examine herself from an external perspective, since she looks at herself as if she were another. Murphy directs attention to the ambiguity thus created by this distancing technique: "This distancing technique is a narratological illustration of the deconstructive nature of Duras' work in general where something is posited (in this instance, autobiography) only to be put into question (autobiography or novel?)."[81] An example of the omniscient narration of Duras' adolescence can be found in the following scene in which the narrator describes the image of the young girl on the ferry-boat:

> Quinze ans et demi. Le corps est mince, presque chétif, des seins d'enfant encore, fardée en rose pâle et en rouge. Et puis cette tenue qui pourrait faire qu'on en rie et dont personne ne rit. (29)

This scene stands in sharp opposition to a prior scene that is told in first-person narration:

> *Que je vous dise encore*, j'ai quinze ans et demie.
> C'est le passage d'un bac sur le Mékong.
> L'image dure pendant toute la traversée du fleuve. (11, my italics)

Typically, this example of first-person narration begins with a brief metacommentary, a brief dialogue with the narratee-reader ("vous")[82], referring to the already told, the fact that she was fifteen and a half when she first encountered the Northern Chinese lover on the ferry-boat. In effect, in this metacommentary, she is calling attention to her narrating process as she reaffirms details from her past. Contrasting these first- and third-person narrative accounts of the same scene allows

Duras to distance herself from her text and also allows her to show that the nature of
memory itself is under interrogation. To further confirm this viewpoint, one needs
only to continue reading the first of the two above-mentioned scenes:

> Je vois bien que tout est là. Tout est là et rien n'est encore joué, je la
> vois dans les yeux, tout est déjà dans les yeux. Je veux écrire. Déjà
> je l'ai dit à ma mère: ce que je veux c'est ça, écrire. (29)

Duras switches from the third-person narration back to the first-person narration in
order to justify her memory process since the first-person narration takes an
adamantly defensive position about what it remembers. A variant of how Duras
combines first-person narration and third-person narration to tell the young girl's
story is the following:

> Je regardais ce qu'il faisait de moi, comme il se servait de moi
> et je n'avais jamais pensé qu'on pouvait le faire de la sorte, il allait au-
> delà de mon espérance et conformément à la destinée de mon corps.
> Ainsi j'étais devenue son enfant. Il était devenu autre chose aussi
> pour moi. Je commençais à reconnaître la douceur inexprimable de
> sa peau, de son sexe, au-delà de lui-même. ... J'étais devenue son
> enfant. C'était avec son enfant qu'il faisait l'amour chaque soir. Et
> parfois il prend peur, tout à coup il s'inquiète de sa santé comme s'il
> découvrait qu'elle était mortelle et que l'idée le traversait qu'il pouvait
> la perdre. (122)

Here the reason for the switch from first-person narration to third-person narration
is almost certainly to create a shift in focus from internal to external in order to place
more emphasis on the Northern Chinese lover and his feelings of fear about losing
"his child"- whether it be through her death or through her return to France. Hewitt
offers: "Her doubled subject (I/she) draws her strength from the myriad
identifications with others' desires, rather than from the presumption of a unique,
undivided self, impervious to others' demands."[83] In this manner, eclipsing the first-
person view allows for the needs of others to manifest themselves so as to render a

more extensive portrayal of herself. Duras does not give a fixed impression of herself as seen by herself; points of view other than that of Duras, the author-identified narrator, are presented. This is not the only time when Duras combines external third-person points of view with her personal voice. The scene where, as a child, she is physically beaten by her mother permits us to further analyze this technique of switching back and forth between the first- and third-person narrations in order to place the emphasis on someone else:

> Derrière les murs de la chambre fermée, le frère.
> Le frère répond à la mère, il lui dit qu'elle a raison de battre l'enfant, sa voix est feutrée, intime, caressante, il lui dit qu'il leur faut savoir la vérité, à n'importe quel prix, il leur faut la savoir pour empêcher que la mère en soit désespérée. La mère frappe de toutes ses forces. Le petit frère crie à la mère de la laisser tranquille. Il va dans le jardin, il se cache, il a peur que je sois tuée, il a peur, il a toujours peur de cet inconnu, notre frère aîné. La peur du petit frère calme ma mère. Elle pleure sur le désastre de sa vie, de son enfant déshonorée. Je pleure avec elle. (73-74)

In this example, Duras is able, via her manipulation of narrative voices, to emphasize not only her own shame but the older brother's maliciousness, the mother's anger, and the fear of the older brother that she and her younger brother shared. Moreover, as Margaret Sankey has pointed out in her article, "Time and Autobiography in *L'Amant* by Marguerite Duras," the switch from first- to third-person narration entails a shift in focus from a desiring subject to an object of desire. Sankey cites the following example, found at the end of *L'Amant*, where the young Duras is separated from her lover:

> Elle aussi c'était lorsque le bateau avait lancé son premier adieu, quand on avait relevé la passerelle et que les remorqueurs avaient commencé à la tirer, à l'éloigner de la terre, qu'elle avait pleuré. (135)

In analyzing this example, Sankey explains: "Benveniste talks about the third person as being an absent non-person, someone who is talked *about* in contrast to the presence in the enunciation of I/you. This takes on a particular meaning in the context of this text as it makes explicit the distance that the narrator feels with this moment of herself."[84] By switching from the first- to third-person narration, Duras moves the emphasis from the desiring subject "je" and places it on "elle," the object of her own desire, while at the same time achieving the emotional distance that she needs. Sankey also points out that the use of the pluperfect tense helps to reinforce this distance since it cuts off all continuity with the present.[85]

With this manipulation of narrative voices, Duras also achieves both an internal and external reexamination of her past self so that she not only actively reexamines her past self but conceptualizes as well how she was seen by others as she becomes the object of their gaze. For example, again in the passage where Duras, principally from the external perspective of third-person narration, gives a physical description of the fifteen-and-a-half-year-old adolescent as she was first seen on the ferry-boat, we see:

> Quinze ans et demi. Le corps est mince. presque chétif, des seins d'enfant encore, fardée en rose pâle et en rouge. Et puis cette tenue qui pourrait faire qu'on en rie et dont personne ne rit. Je vois bien que tout est là. ...
>
> *La petite au chapeau de feutre est dans la lumière limoneuse du fleuve, seule sur le pont du bac, accoudée au bastingage. Le chapeau d'homme colore de rose toute la scène.* (29-30, my italics)

This scene is important to the unfolding of the narration for, in presenting a physical description of the young Duras from the external perspective of a third-person narration, it has the effect of giving the reader the impression of looking through Duras' eyes as she contemplates the imaginary photograph of herself. It is, in effect, Duras' narcissistic gaze at herself. As readers, we thus have the feeling of observing

Duras' past from an objective point of view that is external to Duras herself. Or in reading this scene, we as readers may have the impression of looking through the eyes of the Northern Chinese lover as he scrutinizes the girl. In analyzing this passage, Hewitt writes: "Subject identity is articulated through the concomitant, inseparable processes of identification and alienation. To evidence the already (distanced) identification in the image, the narrator, using the third person, continually takes her distance from the image, looks at it as would someone else, as if it were someone else."[86]

Another aspect of the ability to switch back and forth between the first- and third-person narrations is the use of direct discourse, the type of discourse which renders verbatim what a character says. The use of direct discourse heightens mimetic illusion as the reader no longer feels that the omniscient narrator is acting as an editor who reworks a character's speech or thoughts. On the contrary, the reader feels closer to the text as there is less distance between her/himself and the characters since the narrator is acting as a reporter who gives verbatim accounts of the characters' speech and thoughts. For example, when presenting her mother's conversation with the head of her boarding house, Duras uses direct discourse:

> Ma mère a dit à la directrice de la pension: ça ne fait rien, tout
> ça c'est sans importance, vous avez vu? ces petites robes usées, ce
> chapeau rose et ces souliers en or, comme cela lui va bien? (112)

It is possible that the reader would find it bothersome that Duras uses direct discourse in an autobiography when it is not clear as to whether or not she was a witness to the conversation. How is Duras able to report the exact words of her mother if she was not a witness? Did her mother or the head of her boarding house tell her what had been said during the conversation, thereby setting up a communication network? However, the reader's uneasiness is somewhat alleviated when Duras switches from the first- to third-person narration as she completes the description of the scene (note that the first-person account begins the narration in the past tense and that the third-person narration switches tenses to use the present tense):

> La mère est ivre de joie quand elle parle de ses enfants et alors son charme est encore plus grand. Les jeunes surveillantes de la pension écoutent la mère passionnément. Tous, dit la mère, ils tournent autour de ça, ils veulent de cette petite, de cette chose-là, pas tellement définie encore, regardez, encore une enfant. Déshonorée disent les gens? et moi je dis: comment ferait l'innocence pour se déshonorer? (112-113)

Since the reader assumes that the narrator is omniscient or all-knowing, the question of whether or not Duras was present at the time of this conversation between her mother and the head of the boarding house is less problematic. In this way, Duras, by employing both the first- and third-person narrations, gives the impression of being able to overcome one of the difficulties of autobiographers -- that of the credibility of directly quoted dialogues. Furthermore, by using both first- and third-person narrations, Duras is able present the mother's point of view and, indeed, actual words are given to amplify the description of the adolescent. Nonetheless, the reader will continue to question the validity of this description as s/he wonders if this is a true description given by the mother or the head of the boarding house and remembered by the daughter or an imaginary construction of the self.

To sum up, by switching back and forth between the first-person narration of her remembered adolescence and the third-person narration of the young Duras as seen by the omniscient narrator, Duras is able to show multiple levels of her identity within the boundaries of the "autobiographical space"of *L'Amant*. By means of the shift between these two distinct types of narration, the writer is able to distance herself from her text, justify her memory process via the firm and resolute stance of first-person narration, and transfer the dramatic emphasis to others who were a part of her adolescence in order to give a more ample self-portrayal. This ample self-portrayal is enhanced as Duras shows how she affected those surrounding her, focusing on how she saw herself as well as how she imagined she was seen by others as she became the object of others' gazes or of an external perspective, and employing direct discourse.

The omniscient third-person narration of the older Duras, although less prominent than the two other types of narration, is equally important to Duras' autobiographical writing process as it extends her interweaving of verb tenses and different time periods. An example of this second type of third-person narration, is found near the end of *L'Amant*:

> Elle ne sait pas combien de temps après ce départ de la jeune fille blanche il a exécuté l'ordre du père, quand il a fait ce mariage qu'il lui ordonnait de faire avec la jeune fille désignée par les familles depuis dix ans, couverte d'or, elle aussi, des diamants, du jade. Une Chinoise elle aussi originaire du nord, de la ville de Fou-Chouen, venue accompagnée de famille. (140)

In this case, the first "elle" is the older Duras as seen by the omniscient narrator who, as author, fails to recall how long it was after the departure of the "jeune fille blanche" (subject of the other type of third-person narration) that the lover married the Chinese girl. Duras demands here an active participation on the part of the reader[87] as the reader is forced to distinguish between the "elle" of the older Duras and the "jeune fille blanche" of her younger self. The reader must also distinguish between the "elle" of the older Duras, the "elle" of her younger self, and the "elle" of the young wife of the Northern Chinese lover. A little further on, the narrator comments:

> Peut-être connaissait-elle l'existence de la jeune fille blanche. Elle avait des servantes natives de Sadec qui connaissaient l'histoire et qui avaient dû parler. Elle ne devait pas ignorer sa peine. Elles auraient dû être du même âge toutes les deux, seize ans. Cette nuit-là avait-elle vu pleurer son époux? Et, ce voyant, l'avait-elle consolé? ... Qui sait? Peut-être qu'elle se trompait, peut-être avait-elle pleuré

avec lui, sans un mot, le reste de la nuit. Et puis qu'ensuite serait
venu l'amour, après les pleurs.
    Elle, la jeune fille blanche, elle n'avait jamais rien su de ces
événements-là. (141)

This paragraph must be carefully read as the interplay between the three "elles" is
complex, often nebulous. The "elle" of "Peut-être qu'elle se trompait" is the older
Duras as the omniscient narrator hypothesizes about Duras' remembering process
since Duras herself would be incapable of knowing what occurred between the lover
and his young wife ("avait-elle pleuré avec lui?"). This hypothesizing about the
memory process, via an improbable juxtaposition of different points of view, by the
omniscient narrator is reinforced by the final comment that the omniscient narrator
makes about the "elle" as the young Duras: "Elle, la jeune fille blanche, elle n'avait
jamais rien su de ces événements-là." Thus Marguerite Duras, as simultaneous author
and autobiographer, calls our attention to what an autobiographer is truly capable of
remembering and explains why an autobiographer can only provide possible
hypotheses concerning events to which she was not a witness. Duras has resolved
this problem of hypothesizing by an autobiographer by bringing in the omniscient
narrator to comment on the young Duras and the older Duras and then by using this
technique to introduce other points of view. Although it seems that Duras is
fictionalizing her autobiography, to borrow Carol Murphy's terminology, she is
exploring, within an "autobiographical space," the different possible points of view
that come into being as one reexamines one's life.

    The sharp contrast created by beginning *L'Amant* with the first-person
narration and by ending it with the third-person narration of the aged Duras further
illustrates Duras' ability to use both first- and third-person narrations in the same text.
L'Amant opens in a "traditional" autobiographical manner with the focus on Duras
herself. She comments, in the first-person narration combined with directly quoted
discourse, on the fact that one day a man came up to her and told her that he prefered
her ravaged face of old age to the beautiful face of her youth. This comment on

Duras' recent past leads into the narration of Duras' affair with the Northern Chinese lover which is continually mixed with unspecified periods of time in Duras' present, recent past, and far past. Therefore, it is not surprising that Duras ends *L'Amant* with an annotation on her recent past since throughout the whole of *L'Amant*, there has been a constant mixture of time levels. In addition, the recent past ending brings the reader back to Duras' present. Yet, by ending *L'Amant* with the third-person narration, Duras prevents the final emphasis from being just on herself, allowing for the reader to be exposed more directly to the pain suffered by the Northern Chinese lover. To be more precise, Duras ends *L'Amant* with the narration of the telephone call, after many years had passed, from her Northern Chinese lover:

> Des années après la guerre, après les mariages, les enfants, les divorces, les livres, il était venu à Paris avec sa femme. Il lui avait téléphoné. C'est moi. Elle l'avait reconnu dès la voix. Elle avait dit: c'est moi, bonjour. Il était intimidé, il avait peur comme avant. Sa voix tremblait tout à coup. Et avec le tremblement, tout à coup, elle avait retrouvé l'accent de la Chine. Il savait qu'elle avait commencé à écrire des livres, il l'avait su par la mère qu'il avait revue à Saigon. Et aussi pour le petit frère, qu'il avait été triste pour elle. Et puis il n'avait plus su quoi lui dire. Et puis il le lui avait dit. Il lui avait dit que c'était comme avant, qu'il l'aimait encore, qu'il ne pourrait jamais cesser de l'aimer, qu'il l'aimerait jusqu'à sa mort. (141-142)

Duras could have ended *L'Amant* by using the first-person narration and by directly quoting the Northern Chinese lover's words as she did with the man's words at the beginning of the book. Instead, she chooses to use the third-person narration of the aged Duras which places stress on the Northern Chinese lover, highlighting his need to tell her that he would always love her. The focus of the final passsage is clearly on the Northern Chinese lover since the first "C'est moi" (rendered in the form of direct discourse without quotation marks) is attributed to him. This final episode of Duras' autobiography, not only shows the pain suffered by her lover but its decisive significance in her life as well for it was this telephone call that served as the catalyst for her need to write *L'Amant*. Readers of *L'Amant* should note the distinction between the Northern Chinese lover's apparently documented or real telephone call that served as the catalyst for Duras' need to write *L'Amant* and the imaginary photograph that was the "creative catalyst" for Duras' autobiographical writing process in *L'Amant*.

In juxtaposing first-person narration with the two types of third-person narration, Duras subtly employs other narrative techniques. For example, an interesting aspect of the third-person narration of the young Duras as seen by the omniscient narrator is the imperative manner in which the omniscient narrator will direct questions to the narratee, the implied reader inscribed within the narrative text,[88] concerning the young Duras. The following example illustrates how Duras' affair with the Northern Chinese lover and her family's reaction to it had become the subject of gossip:

> Quinze ans et demi. La chose se sait très vite dans le poste de Sadec. Rien que cette tenue dirait le déshonneur. La mère n'a aucun sens de rien, ni celui de la façon d'élever une petite fille. La pauvre enfant. Ne croyez pas ce chapeau n'est pas innocent, ni ce rouge à lèvres, tout ça signifie quelque chose, ce n'est pas innocent, ça veut dire, c'est pour attirer les regards, l'argent. Les frères, des voyous. On dit que c'est un Chinois, le fils du milliardaire, la villa de Mékong, en céramiques bleues. Même lui, au lieu d'en être honoré, il n'en veut pas pour son fils. Famille de voyous blancs. (108-109)

In this passage, beginning with "Ne croyez pas ce chapeau n'est pas innocent," the quasi direct discourse, a form of *style indirect libre* or "seemingly indirect style" is used. The omniscient narrator adopts the speech characteristics of those people who would be gossiping about the young Duras, her behavior, and her family. Her use of the imperative ("ne croyez pas") incorporates the narratee. In so doing, the omniscient narrator forces the actual reader of the text to become more involved in the reading process. It is via this relay between the narrator and the narratee, that the actual reader becomes more acutely aware of the tension on the part of the narrator in her efforts to accurately relate the events of Duras' adolescence. This technique also gives the reader the impression that questions that s/he would like to have asked about the young Duras' reputation have been answered. Duras will also incorporate the narratee when using first-person narration. For example, in the following passage, the narrator is directing the narrative to a specific type of narratee:

> Ce n'est donc pas à la cantine de Réam, vous voyez, comme je l'avais écrit, que je rencontre l'homme riche à la limousine noire, c'est après, sur le bac, ce jour que je raconte, dans cette lumière de brume et de chaleur. (36)

In this passage, the narrator presupposes that the narratee is familiar with the other narratives that this narrator has told. The narrator is directing the narrative to a particular narratee -- one that will perfectly understand and completely approve of the least of the narrator's words and the most subtle of the narrator's intentions. The concept of intertextuality is important here since Duras, the author-identified narrator, is directly pointing out that she is making an intertextual reference or more specifically, a correction in her autobiography of a detail that she had previously written about in one of her "autofictional narratives."

The concept of "autobiographical space" encompasses the image of the self across many genres or across all the works of an author. This is especially true in the case of Duras since to believe that the whole of her work is inspired by autobiographical facts has become commonplace. She enjoyed using her own life story as the foundation for her novels and placed prime importance on the role of the imagination since it enabled her to continue to explore new directions in her writing. Essentially, she used the technique of writing and rewriting the same memories at various points in her life as a means of gradually recovering her past. For Duras, the role of memory is crucial since it alters the selection process, especially as one ages and one has more time to reflect upon the events of one's life.

Yet, to determine the place of *L'Amant* in relation to her other "autofictional narratives" is not easily done. It has in fact become an intricate process. Aliette Armel, in her article "Le jeu autobiographique," warns: "Mais dès la page 14 de *l'Amant*, une affirmation péremptoire met en doute la part de vérité contenue dans cette démarche autobiographique: 'L'histoire de ma vie n'existe pas'. ... *L'Amant*, contrairement aux conclusions issues d'une lecture trop rapide, se situerait donc dans la continuité directe du reste de l'oeuvre, au coeur de laquelle se retrouvent le silence et l'absence, et l'autobiographie ne serait qu'un moyen, mis au service de l'écriture qui seule donne une quelconque valeur d'existence aux événements anecdotiques qu'elle rapporte."[89] Duras herself maintains in *La Vie matérielle*, while commenting on the autobiographical writing process, that her life story is constantly pulverized by the present:

> Mon histoire, elle est pulvérisée chaque seconde de chaque jour, par le présent de la vie, et je n'ai aucune possibilité d'apercevoir clairement ce qu'on appelle ainsi: sa vie. ... Je me demande sur quoi se basent les gens pour raconter leur vie. C'est vrai qu'il y a tellement de modèles de récits qui sont faits à partir de celui de la chronologie, des faits extérieurs. On prend ce modèle-là en général. On part du commencement de sa vie et sur les rails des événements, les guerres, les changements d'adresse, les mariages, on descend vers le présent.[90]

Furthermore, she reiterates in a detailed interview with Hervé Le Masson of *Le Nouvel Observateur* what she had inscribed as a metacommentary in *L'Amant*: "L'histoire de votre vie, de ma vie, elles n'existent pas, ou bien alors il s'agit de lexicologie. Le roman de ma vie, de nos vies, oui, mais pas l'histoire. C'est dans la reprise des temps par l'imaginaire que le souffle est rendu à la vie."[91] It appears that *L'Amant* is only a part of the continuum of Duras' work. Yet even Duras herself realized the value attributed to the change created by *L'Amant*. In a televised interview on September 28, 1984 with Bernard Pivot, commentator of the literary program "Apostrophes," she admitted: "C'est la première fois que je n'écris pas une fiction."[92] Duras thus sees *L'Amant* as the success of a new form of writing, no longer a novel or a work of fiction. This is further confirmed by her statement to Gilles Costaz of *Le Matin* where she states that her dream of attaining *l'écriture courante* has been fulfilled in writing *L'Amant*:

> J'ai toujours rêvé de ce que j'appelle l'écriture courante, sans jamais l'atteindre vraiment et tout à coup, justement sans le vouloir, sans rien vouloir d'autre que de m'en tenir à la précision de la mémoire, je l'atteignais et je ressentais que je l'atteignais.[93]

Pieces of paratextual information that concern *L'Amant* and the more recent "autofictional narrative" *L'Amant de la Chine du nord* are illuminating for understanding how Duras achieved her dream of *l'écriture courante*. In the detailed interview with Hervé Le Masson of *Le Nouvel Observateur*, she explains that an imaginary photograph, a remembered image from her childhood, was the creative origin for *L'Amant*:

> Oui. Le texte de "L'Amant" s'est d'abord appelé "L'image absolue."
> Il devait courir tout au long d'un album de photographies de mes films et de moi. Cette image, cette photographie absolue non photographiée est entrée dans le livre.[94]

In this same detailed interview, Duras mentions her reasons for resuscitating this image of when she was fifteen and a half and on a ferry crossing the Mekong River:

> Au moment où la photo aurait pu être prise, personne ne savait l'importance de ce passage du bac. Ça a été le déclenchement de la vie. C'est après, pour la première fois, que j'ai menti à ma mère, sur cet amour-là, c'est-à-dire, sur mon propre désir.[95]

Duras' need to write *L'Amant* was stimulated by this photograph of her imagination. In an explicit manner, this need is inscribed directly in the text of *L'Amant*:

C'est au cours de ce voyage que l'image se serait détachée, qu'elle aurait été enlevée à la somme. Elle aurait pu exister, une photographie aurait pu être prise, comme une autre, ailleurs, dans d'autres circonstances. Mais elle ne l'a pas été. L'objet était trop mince pour la provoquer. Qui aurait pu penser à ça? Elle n'aurait pu être prise que si on avait pu préjuger de l'importance de cet événement dans ma vie, cette traversée du fleuve. (16-17)

Here, Duras has produced an image of herself that respects her actual past, the image of a photograph that never existed, that never was taken but nonetheless sets in motion autobiographical confession. As such, it points to the complex interdependence of imagination and truth, in which the powerful role assigned to the imagination raises doubts about truth. Perhaps this is an inevitable outcome of a text that mixes autobiographical fact and invented images. For Duras, however, it is more than this: it is a matter of finding again the traces left in oneself by the past, transformed by time, memory, and imagination. She thus strives for and attains a more personal truth as she includes multiple elements, even lies. Armel, when discussing the significance of finding again these traces, affirms: "La vérité que l'on atteint ainsi est qualifiée par Marguerite Duras de 'personnelle' car elle inclut des éléments multiples sans exclure, même, le mensonge. C'est la seule connaissance possible que l'on peut avoir de soi, la seule façon de rendre compte au présent, par l'écrit, de son histoire personnelle: cette vérite dépasse alors la description d'un itinéraire individuel pour atteindre à l'universel, à ce que Marguerite Duras appelle 'l'ensemble'."[96]

Just as the imaginary photograph was the creative catalyst for *L'Amant*, Jean-Jacques Annaud's film *The Lover* triggered Duras' need to write *L'Amant de la Chine du nord*. Initially the 1991 publication of *L'Amant de la Chine du nord* was widely criticized. Some claimed Duras was in financial difficulty and consequently was trying to cash in on the continued success of *L'Amant* by sacrificing her literary talent. Still others maintained that because Duras had had a bitter falling out with Annaud, she wrote *L'Amant de la Chine du nord* to steal the limelight from his film.

However, my aim is to show that since Annaud's film *The Lover* was not pleasing to Duras, it resulted in her need to write *L'Amant de la Chine du nord* that included indications for the direction of a film and direct references to her other works.

Paratextual information on the origins of *L'Amant de la Chine du nord* can be found in Duras' comment in its preface: after stating that she now has written the story of the lover from Northern China and the child, which had not yet been there in *L'Amant* ("J'ai écrit l'histoire de l'amant de la Chine du Nord et de l'enfant: elle n'était pas encore là dans *l'Amant,* ...["97]"), Duras declares: "Je suis redevenue un écrivain de romans." (12) This comment emphasizes how Duras has enjoyed using her own life story as the foundation for her novels and how the role of the imagination is of prime importance to her. As was previously stated, she had in fact admitted in the televised interview with Bernard Pivot that in writing *L'Amant,* she had, for the first time, not written a piece of fiction. Knowing that the imagination is a key element in Duras' writing, it is possible to hypothesize that Duras felt the need to return to her fictional writing in order to reexamine better her past life.

However, while indeed *L'Amant de la Chine du nord* appears at first to be a rewriting or revision of *L'Amant,* there are some crucial differences between the two works and the two works do form integral parts of the continuum of her creative autobiographical writing process. First of all, stylistically *L'Amant* is made up of both first- and third-person narrations juxtaposed with the intertwining of verb tenses and different time periods to create a non-chronological narrative. In contrast, the technically more complex *L'Amant de la Chine du nord* consists of two types of third-person narration in a chronologically ordered text with footnotes and an appendix for film directions. To be more specific, in the footnotes and in the appendix, Duras gives instructions which reflect her desire to reproduce the same effect of distance in a film as in the text of *L'Amant de la Chine du nord.*

Moreover, Duras includes several intertextual references to *L'Amant* and to her other "autofictional narratives" that firmly reinforce the belief that Duras has carefully constructed an "autobiographical space" that encompasses the image of the self across many genres and across all of her works. For example, at the very beginning of *L'Amant de la Chine du nord*, the omniscient narrator states: "Elle, c'est celle qui n'a de nom dans le premier livre ni dans celui qui l'avait précédé ni dans celui-ci." (13) Here, "le premier livre" refers to *L'Amant* and "celui qui l'avait précédé" refers to an "autofictional narrative" that preceded *L'Amant*. Secondly, the two books offer different perspectives on their protagonist-author. In *L'Amant*, the omniscient narrator refers to the young Duras as "la jeune fille blanche" and in *L'Amant de la Chine du nord*, the omniscient narrator refers to the young Duras as "la petite." It would seem then in using "la petite" to reflect maternally on her younger self, Duras is echoing her mother's voice when speaking about her daughter. And thirdly, there is a common difference in emphasis in the two books. In general, I find that *L'Amant* tends to concentrate mainly on the mother's anger, the evilness of the hoodlum older brother, and the lover's fragile personality. In contrast, *L'Amant de la Chine du nord* focuses on the relationship between the lover and the child, a relationship in conflict with the child's desire for the younger brother Paulo. Furthermore, *L'Amant de la Chine du nord* emphasizes the strong but tender personality of the lover, especially when in confrontation with the older brother Pierre. For example, in *L'Amant*, the following description of the lover centers on his fragility, his lack of masculinity:

> La peau est d'une somptueuse douceur. Le corps. Le corps est maigre, sans force, sans muscles, il pourrait avoir été malade, être en convalescence, il est imberbe, sans virilité autre que celle du sexe, il est très faible, il paraît être à la merci d'une insulte, souffrant. (49)

In contrast, the following description from *L'Amant de la Chine du nord* shows his strength:

> Le Chinois lâche l'enfant. Il traverse la piste de danse. Il

s'avance vers le frère aîné attablé à côté de la mère. Il s'approche très près de lui. Il le regarde trait après trait comme s'il était passionnément intéressé.

Le frère aîné prend peur. (159)

Nevertheless, one wonders why Duras was impelled to write a new version of the story of the lover from Northern China and the child, a version with new details and circumstances, indications for the direction of a film, and direct references to other Durasian works. It does not simply seem to be a question of returning to the form of the novel. Part of the answer to the intertextual play between these works is found in a detailed interview with Duras and her companion Yann Andréa that was conducted by Leslie Garis of *The New York Times Magazine*. The discussion on *L'Amant de la Chine du nord* was as follows:

"Let me tell you something," she says. Her voice is gruff, energetic and frank. "I am finishing a book. I am going to pick up the story of *The Lover* without any literature in it. The fault I have found with *The Lover* was its literariness, which comes very easily to me because it's my style. But you won't understand that."
"Even I am struggling to understand," says Yann, smiling. "Another version of *The Lover* without the style of *The Lover*? It's the same story."
"Not exactly. Another novel. It is between the little girl and the Chinese."
"Why go over the material again?" I (Leslie Garis) ask.
"Because there is a film maker who is one of the greatest in the world, whose name is Jean-Jacques Annaud, who took on *The Lover*. He told a story that I didn't recognize, so I said: 'Now you're going home, its finished. I don't want to work with you anymore.' I was a little nasty."[98]

This piece of paratextual information allows us to infer that because Annaud created a film version of *L'Amant* that was not pleasing to Duras, it resulted in her need to write *L'Amant de la Chine du nord*.[99] It is helpful to consider that certain film critics, as for example Daniel Toscan du Plantier, support Duras' displeasure with the film:

"En publiant récemment sa propre réécriture de son livre, sous le titre de *L'Amant de la Chine du nord*, Marguerite Duras a répondu à la nécessaire dépossession de son premier travail, éloigné d'elle par le passage du cinéma. Il ne sert à rien de dire que le film *L'Amant* n'est pas, ne peut être le livre transposé par un coup de baguette magique sur la surface de l'écran. Il a fallu renoncer à l'essentiel, la subjectivité absolue de cette histoire, qui n'a pas d'autre lieu, d'autre mémoire que les mots de l'auteur."[100] Finally, it is also interesting to note the fact that Duras thought there was too much "literature" in *L'Amant*. In developing *L'Amant de la Chine du nord*, Duras implies that she is yet again exploring new directions in her writing.

Chief among Duras' innovative writing strategies in "writing the self" is her use of purposeful shifts in narrative voice. Already shown is the importance of the shifts between first-person narration and the two types of third-person narrations in *L'Amant*, but it is equally important to examine the timely juxtaposition of two types of third-person narration at the end of *L'Amant de la Chine du nord*, since this technique demonstrates Duras' success at showing different points of view and how these points of view can be altered by the passing of time. In the following example, Duras juxtaposes third-person narration by the omniscient narrator, contrasting the remembering process of the older Duras with that of the young Duras who is about to leave colonial French Indochina for France:

> Elle se souvient.
> Devant elle, accoudée au bastingage, il y avait cette fille brune qui regardait également la mer et qui, comme elle, pleurait de tout, de rien.
> Elle se souvient de ça qu'elle avait oublié. (218)

In this example, the omniscient narrator illustrates the ability to shift from one time period to another as she juxtaposes her narrations of the older Duras remembering her departure from colonial French Indochina ("Elle se souvient.") with her narration of the young protagonist who is in the process of departing from colonial French

Indochina ("Devant elle, accoudée au bastingage, ..."). By juxtaposing these two temporal moments, Duras reveals to the reader the two-fold process of the author of an "autofictional narrative": the process by which the author will first remember a certain past event, and then, attribute it to the protagonist of an "autofictional narrative." Duras achieves a similar process in *L'Amant* by juxtaposing the first-person narration with the two types of third-person narration but, in this case, she also uses the juxtaposition for the purpose of making clear the complexities of the memory process of the autobiographical author.

In addition to shifts in narrative voice, essential to Duras' process of "writing the self" is the role of memory since it will alter the selection process, especially as one has aged and has had more time to reflect upon the events of one's life. Duras thus uses the technique of writing and rewriting the same memories at various points in her life as a means of gradually recovering her past. For Duras, retelling creates the opportunity to layer in changes in emotional perspective from a newly learned point of view or from a point of view that is more mature, more able to rationally cope with and understand earlier memory. So, in retelling the same event in various works, Duras achieves different ways of making sense of her life. Suzette A. Henke, in *Shattered Subjects: Trauma and Testsimony in Women's Life-Writing*, has coined the term "scriptotheraphy": "the process of writing out and writing through traumatic experience of therapeutic reenactment ... the authorial effort to reconstruct a story of psychological debilitation could offer potential for mental healing and begin to alleviate persistent symptoms of numbing, dysphoria, and uncontrollable flashbacks."[101] If this term were to be applied to Duras' work, it would appear that her creative endeavors enabled her to come to terms with painful memories of her past.

Thus, *L'Amant de la Chine du nord* is not just a rewriting or revision of *L'Amant* but an integral part of Duras' autobiographical writing process. As a first example, one has only to examine how her mother's racism affected her characterization of her lover. M. Jo, the European lover of *Un Barrage contre le*

Pacifique is the Northern Chinese lover in *L'Amant*. Because her mother was racist, Duras was inhibited about identifying her lover as Northern Chinese, despite his wealth, until after her mother's death. Duras thus states:

> Dans "le Barrage", je lui rendais un hommage qu'elle n'a pas vu, qu'elle n'a pas lu. Pour elle, dans le livre j'accusais sa défaite, je la dénonçais. Qu'elle n'ait pas compris cela reste une des tristesses de ma vie. Ici [*L'Amant*], c'est différent. Il fallait mentir. Mon amant était chinois. Le dire, même dans un livre, ce n'était pas possible du vivant de ma mère. Un Chinois - amant de son enfant - même remarquablement riche, c'était l'équivalent d'une déchéance peut-être encore plus grave que celle de la ruine des barrages parce qu'elle atteignait ce qu'elle vivait comme étant un don du ciel, sa race, ici, blanche.[102]

Changing what she wrote in *Un Barrage contre le Pacifique*, Duras eventually addresses the matter of her family's racism when she revisits the relationship in *L'Amant*. My emphasis here is on the family's racism rather than on Duras' style or technique. For Duras' family, the Northern Chinese lover is an outsider who is tolerated only for his money:

> Les rencontres avec la famille ont commencé avec les grands repas à Cholen. ...
> Mes frères ne lui adresseront jamais la parole. C'est comme s'il n'était pas assez dense pour être perçu, vu, entendu par eux. Cela parce qu'il est à mes pieds, qu'il est posé en principe que je ne l'aime pas, que je suis avec lui pour l'argent, que je ne peux pas l'aimer, que c'est impossible, qu'il pourrait tout supporter de moi sans être jamais au bout de cet amour. Cela, parce que c'est un Chinois, que ce n'est pas un blanc. La façon qu'a ce frère aîné de se taire et d'ignorer l'existence de mon amant procède d'une telle conviction qu'elle en est exemplaire. Nous prenons tous modèle sur le frère aîné face à cet amant. (63-65)

Indeed, the force of the family's racism, especially that of the older brother, is so strong that when the young Duras is surrounded by her family, she feels embarrassed by her Northern Chinese lover and begins to act indifferently to him in their presence. The young Duras will use the family's racist vocabulary in order not to be beaten by her mother:

> Elle [la mère] pleure sur le désastre de sa vie, de son enfant déhonorée. Je pleure avec elle. Je mens. Je jure sur ma vie que rien ne m'est arrivé, rien même pas un baiser. Comment veux-tu, je dis, avec un Chinois, comment veux-tu que je fasse ça avec un Chinois, si laid, si malingre? (74)

In *L'Amant de la Chine du nord*, Duras once again takes up the question of the family's racism towards her lover. However, this time she shows it via a conversation between the lover and the child:

> Le Chinois dit en souriant:
> – Quand ils sont là tu ne m'aimes pas.
> Elle prend sa main, l'embrasse. Elle dit:
> – Je ne peux pas savoir. J'ai voulu que tu les voies une fois
> dans ta vie. C'est vrai, peut-être, que leur présence m'empêche de te
> voir ici. (152)

Here, because direct discourse is used, we are able to perceive the lover's consciousness of the change in attitude that occurs in the child when in the presence of her family. Therefore, by comparing the change in role for M. Jo from a European lover in *Un Barrage contre le Pacifique* to a Northern Chinese lover in *L'Amant* to a more active role in *L'Amant de la Chine du nord*, we are able to chart Duras' increasing sensitivity to her family's racism and we note how she was only able to talk more fully about it when the danger of her family suffering from the revelation of her affair had passed.

We can see another example of how Duras' own maturity yields new or clearer insights when she reanalyzes aspects of her past in her treatment of her relationship with her brothers. In *L'Amant*, she speaks of her two brothers - the mean older brother and the fragile younger one. In *L'Amant de la Chine du nord*, Duras again writes of two brothers but this time she also depicts the constant fear that the older brother would kill the younger brother, the older brother's fear of the Northern Chinese lover and the child's desire for the younger brother. For example, in *L'Amant de la Chine du nord*, Duras portrays a scene of incest between the child and Paulo, the fragile younger brother. Note in this example the effect of distancing oneself from painful memories created by the use of third-person narration:

> Paulo était venu dans la salle de bains par la petite porte du côté du fleuve. Ils s'étaient embrassés beaucoup. Et puis elle s'était mise nue et puis elle s'était étendue à côté de lui et elle lui avait montré qu'il fallait qu'il vienne sur son corps à elle. Il avait fait ce qu'elle avait dit. Elle l'avait embrassé encore et elle l'avait aidé. (200)

However, in *Un Barrage contre le Pacifique* (1950), Duras speaks of only one brother who is good; and in *L'Eden cinéma* (1988), she describes a mean brother. Hewitt explains:

> This despised older brother is symbolically killed off in *The Sea Wall*: the young girl Suzanne has only one (good) brother. In the context of *The Lover*, the early fiction appears as a dream fulfillment. First of all, the young girl's revolt against a morally bankrupt social system remains ideally pure, since she shuns the advances of the reprehensible Mr. Jo. Next, Duras conveniently has the mother die near the end, thereby freeing son and daughter. Finally, the girl rides off into the sunset with her only brother (whom she idolizes) and his mistress.[103]

This "despised older brother" was such an eminent presence in the young Duras' life that in *L'Amant* she is able to show that her desire for her Northern Chinese lover was severely affected, almost even destroyed by it:

> En présence de mon frère aîné il cesse d'être mon amant. Il ne cesse pas d'exister mais il ne m'est plus rien. Il devient un endroit brûlé. Mon désir obéit à mon frère aîné, il rejette mon amant. (66)

In addition, in *L'Amant de la Chine du nord*, Duras shows that the child's desire for the younger brother is so strong that the Northern Chinese lover becomes jealous of him:

> Elle répète (au Chinois):
> – Je t'ai désiré tout de suite ... très vite très fort à ce moment-là ... c'est vrai.
> – Autant que ton petit frère ...
> Elle réflèchit. Elle dit:
> – Comment dire ça ... *mon petit frère c'est aussi mon enfant* ... (144, my italics)

Thus, it is across the "autobiographical space"of the whole of Duras' work that we are able to understand the different ways that Duras makes sense of her life as we see the progression from the fictitious creation of a happy union between the girl and the brother in *Un Barrage contre le Pacifique* to the ability to acknowledge both brothers in *L'Amant* to the admission of and to a rational coping with the wickedness of the older brother in *L'Eden cinéma* to finally the psychological complexity of sibling relationships in *L'Amant de la Chine du nord* in which, even in the face of danger from the evil older brother, the desire of the child for the younger brother is consummated. Yet, as readers of the continuum of Duras' "autobiographical space," we cannot but help to ask ourselves how do we know if Duras is getting closer to the truth or is she simply exaggerating or creating more lies as she no longer has witnesses to past events. We have no physical or testimonial (other than Duras') proof that incest between the child and Paulo actually occurred. Is this scene of incest an imaginary construct of the self as is the imaginary photograph? Is Duras getting closer to the truth or is it only a question of perception?

A final example of Duras' fruitful capacity to reexamine the same past event in separate works is her study of the relationship between the mother and this "despised older brother," which is characterized by the obsessive love that the mother had for her son. Of the three children, it was always the older brother that the mother favored the most. In *L'Amant*, Duras describes the family atmosphere of her childhood:

> Non seulement aucune fête n'est célébrée dans notre famille, pas d'arbre de Noël, aucun mouchoir brodé, aucune fleur jamais. Mais aucun mort non plus, aucune sépulture, aucune mémoire. Elle seule. Le frère aîné restera un assassin. Le petit frère mourra de ce frère. Moi je suis partie, je me suis arrachée. *Jusqu'à sa mort [celle de la mère] le frère aîné l'a eue pour lui seul.* (72, my italics)

Here, Duras demonstrates her awareness of her mother's obsessive love for her older brother and the pain that she suffered from the fact that her younger brother died unhappily from being under his older brother's domination. In *L'Amant de la Chine du nord*, Duras further analyzes the relationship of the mother and the older brother as she conveys in a conversation between the mother and the Northern Chinese lover about why the mother beats the child (the lover speaks first):

> Ça a duré jusqu'à quand les coups ...
> Jusqu'au jour où Paulo nous a vus tous les trois mon fils et moi enfermés avec la petite dans la chambre. Il ne l'a pas supporté. Il s'est jeté sur lui.
> La mère ajoute:
> Ça a été la plus grande peur de ma vie.
> Le Chinois demande tout bas dans un souffle:
> Vous aviez peur pour lequel de vos fils, Madame?
> La mère regarde le Chinois, elle se lève pour partir puis elle se rassied.
> Le Chinois dit:
> Je vous demande pardon.
> La mère se reprend, elle dit:
> Vous devriez le savoir Monsieur, même l'amour d'un chien, c'est sacré. Et on a ce droit-là -- aussi sacré que celui de vivre -- de n'avoir à en rendre compte à personne. (163)

Here the mother admits that her fixated love for her elder son is sacred and she declares that she is not obligated to explain her reasons for loving her son in such a way to anyone. Yet, paratextually, it is even more interesting to note Duras' careful study on the nature of a mother's obsessive love for her child in "Des journées entières dans les arbres," the first of four short stories in the collection by the same title. From the outset of this concise text, Duras magnifies the intensity of the relationship between the mother and her son Jacques. In the following example, Jacques and his mother are discussing her factory and why she works so hard to manage it properly:

> – Elle marche ton usine? demanda négligemment le fils.
> – Trop. Je mourrai de travailler.
> – Laisse tomber, si c'est pour moi.
> – C'est trop tard, je ne peux pas, et cette idée-là me plaît, c'est désormais la seule idée supportable de ma vie. Je n'ai que toi, je pense à toi, je n'ai pas choisi de t'avoir.[104]

Essentially, Jacques gives meaning to his mother's life. Her obsession with Jacques is so strong that she makes a comparaison between herself and him while talking to Marcelle, Jacques' mistress, in order to explain her reasons for beating him:

> – Il tient de moi, mademoiselle, si vous saviez comme j'étais paresseuse. Une vraie couleuvre. À quinze ans on me retrouvait dans les champs, endormie dans les fossés. Ah! j'aimais ça, flâner, dormir, et d'être dehors, par-dessus tout. Et au début, je vous parle d'il y a vingt ans, quand j'ai vu que Jacques ne faisait toujours rien, je me suis dit que c'était cet instinct-là que j'avais qui lui revenait. Alors j'ai commencé à le battre, à le battre. (29)

Furthermore, so understanding is this mother of her son that she allows him to miss school and spend his entire days in the trees (the mother addresses her son):

> – Des journées entières, tout en haut des branches, on t'appelait, on t'appelait, tu ne répondais pas. Des journées entières ...
> – Remarque, ça ne me déplaisait pas dans un sens ... Les autres travaillaient tellement. Que toi, tu sois dans les arbres, ça ne me

déplaisait pas, ça me changeait, quoi ... (72)

Yet, it is important to point out that Jacques is aware of and not entirely comfortable with his mother's obsessive understanding of him:

Il me restait encore ce témoin *[sa mère]* de ma vie si lâche, pensa-t-il, il faut qu'elle meure, il le faut. (79)

Finally, even after she realizes that Jacques had stolen two of her gold bracelets, the mother explains to Marcelle the depth of her understanding for him:

Rien de lui ne peut tout à fait m'étonner ... en somme, voyez-vous, c'est cela, aussi, retrouver son enfant ... (93)

Duras, in thus creating the fictional characters of Jacques and his mother, is able to further probe into the complexities of the relationship between an obsessive mother and her son.

In conclusion, this chapter has concentrated on Marguerite Duras' efforts to produce a more revealing autobiography through technical manipulation and expansion of the genre as well as on how all of her works are part of the continued development of her "autographical space." Five specific results are achieved from switching back and forth between first- and third-person narration in *L'Amant*: 1.) Duras' ability to distance herself from her text as she designates her alter ego by the indefinite "she;" 2.) the possibility of questioning the nature of memory itself through the point of view of first-person narration, which adamantly justifies the memory process; 3.) the capacity to transfer the dramatic emphasis to others who were a part of her adolescence so as to give a more ample self-portrayal by showing how she affected those surrounding her; 4.) the skill to focus on how she saw herself as well as how she imagines she was seen by others as she becomes the object of others' gazes or of points of view external to hers; and 5.) the freedom to employ direct discourse. Indeed, Duras' texts demand an active participation on the part of the reader in order to follow and interpret her writing strategies. Just as she is both participant and narrator, her texts insist that we participate in the double role of co-author and reader in the autobiographical writing process. Moreover, as an imaginary photograph was the creative catalyst for *L'Amant*, Jean Jacques Annaud's film *The Lover* propelled Duras' creation of *L'Amant de la Chine du nord*. Primary here is how Duras gradually recovers her past through the technique of writing and rewriting the same memories at various points in her life, as she has done in *L'Amant* and in her "autofictional narratives." As we consider the totality of her "auotbiographical space," Duras shows us the great difference between mere repetition and rewriting. With her technical skill and creative expansion of narrative possibilities, Duras makes each account of her childhood not only different but more subtle, fuller, more revealing, and richer than the last.

Marguerite Duras died in Paris on March 3, 1996. She was survived by her son Jean Mascolo. Her last work, *C'est tout* (1995), was comprised of carefully dated self-reflective entries from October 1994 to February 1995. This last work of Duras' was praised by some critics, who admired her refusal to die quietly, and criticized by others, who were shocked by her immodesty.

Chapter Four

Alain Robbe-Grillet's *Le Miroir qui revient*,

Angélique ou l'enchantement, and

Les Derniers jours de Corinthe

> *Autofiction*: "a story in which the author places himself, more or less clearly and more or less by name, in situations which he simultaneously depicts, more or less forcefully, as imaginary or fictitious." – Serge Doubrovsky[105]

Before the publications of *Le Miroir qui revient* (1984), *Angélique ou l'enchantement* (1987), and *Les Derniers jours de Corinthe* (1994), a clear demarcation could be made between Alain Robbe-Grillet's creative work (including both his novels and his films) and his critical work (particularly noteworthy is his *Pour un nouveau roman* [1961]). These three new works are part of a trilogy with the *sur-titre* or "comprehensive title" *Romanesques*. This *sur-titre*, an important piece of paratextual information, forewarns the reader that these texts are neither simply to be taken as *roman*, nor as autobiography. Robbe-Grillet himself clarified the use of *Romanesques* during an interview with Jacques Henric: "Je ne voulais pas écrire *roman* sur ces livres. En même temps je souhaitais que quelque chose du titre indique qu'il s'agissait bien de *fiction* et empêche de classer ces écrits dans la catégorie *autobiographie.*"[106] In the *Romanesques* series, Robbe-Grillet intentionally blurs the distinction between fact and fiction by combining autobiographical elements with fictitious elements and critical theories. In fact, the critical theories, which dominate all three texts, and which are particularly intrusive for the reader in *Angélique ou l'enchantement,*[107] are presented in the form of metacommentaries. Their presence is the most distinctive feature by which the reader differentiates between the three *Romanesques* works and what Robbe-Grillet had previously written, classified by critics under the rubric of the *Nouveau Roman.*

Confronted with the coexistence of these varied elements within the covers of one book in the *Romanesques* trilogy, the reader may be left uncertain as to which genre these works belong. They take us far beyond Lejeune's expanded definition of "autobiographical space" introduced to account for the diverse writing strategies that André Gide used to compose the history of his personality across several works. For Gide, his writing, especially his fictional works, was a source of catharsis, an act of purification.[108] It is not surprising then that Gide had more success at producing an image of the self through his various works than simply through the autobiographical ones. It was predominantly in his fictional works that Gide was able to show the multiple levels of his identity.

However, unlike Gide who created separate texts in order to analyze the various aspects of his personality, Robbe-Grillet developed a unique method of combining several means of studying his personality, his thought, and his life in one text. He achieved this by experimenting with diverse writing strategies that involved the interweaving of fictitious elements and critical theories into an autobiographical narrative. Hence, the *Romanesques* trilogy is not only completely different from what Robbe-Grillet had previously written, but are innovative forms of "writing the self" that demonstrate the need to enlarge Lejeune's concept. Lejeune's concept is, of course, still applicable to those authors who use different writing strategies across several works in order to examine the multiple levels of their identity; however, it needs to be enlarged if it is to include works that use several different writing strategies within the covers of a single text.

Critics have been quick to point out Robbe-Grillet's diverse writing techniques, as is evident in the following assessments of *Le Miroir qui revient* and *Angélique ou l'enchantement*:

> Il y a quelques semaines, dans ces mêmes colonnes, j'ai fait l'éloge du doute (à propos du Journal intime). Je ferai ici celui de l'ambiguïté, à propos du livre d'Alain Robbe-Grillet, *Le Miroir qui revient*, qui revêt une forme proche du Journal, disons une forme cousine, puisque c'est à la fois un livre de souvenirs et un livre de commentaires, je dirais plus précisément une autobiographie sans vérité en même temps qu'une justification sans dogme.[109]; and,

> Roman, essai, autobiographie? Robbe-Grillet, à propos du *Miroir*, s'est déjà expliqué sur ces classifications mais, comme il aime brouiller les cartes, les mêmes questions, à la lecture d'*Angélique ou l'enchantement*, ne vont pas manquer de rebondir. L'auteur, ou plutôt le narrateur car sujet de l'énoncé et sujet de l'énonciation mènent un vertigineux ballet au coeur de la fiction, parle même, cette fois, de "mémoire". Allons-y pour "mémoire", mais n'oublions pas que l'ensemble de la trilogie porte désormais le sur-titre de *Romanesques*.[110]

For the first-time reader of the *Romanesques* trilogy, attention also must be drawn to the description of *Le Miroir qui revient* that is found on the back cover of the text:

> Ce livre d'Alain Robbe-Grillet est fort différent de tout ce qu'il a publié jusqu'ici. Sans doute parce que ce n'est pas un roman. Mais, est-ce vraiment une autobiographie?[111]

This statement, a source of paratextual information, immediately indicates to the reader that Robbe-Grillet is creating a new type of text to describe the self that is neither a traditional autobiography nor a work of pure fiction. Robbe-Grillet's answer to Jean-Pierre Salgas' question as to whether or not he had published his autobiography is also noteworthy:

> Il ne s'agit pas d'une autobiographie, ou alors tous mes écrits le sont. Comme je le dis dans le livre, je n'ai jamais parlé d'autre chose que de moi. Disons qu'il y a, dans *Le Miroir qui revient*, de nombreuses pages qui ont une valeur autobiographique directe. Mais je ne suis pas sûr que l'ensemble respecte le pacte autobiographique, tel que le définit Philippe Lejeune.[112]

A similar statement is present in the text of *Le Miroir qui revient*: "Je n'ai jamais parlé d'autre chose que de moi. Comme c'était de l'intérieur, on ne s'en est guère aperçu."[10] Mireille Calle-Gruber responds to Robbe-Grillet's ambiguous claims with the following:

> Pour ma part, au-delà de la boutade et de la surprise, j'entends prendre au mot cette phrase et interroger alors le curieux statut d'une énonciation qui dit "parler *de l'intérieur*", et d'un sujet qui parle de soi sans qu'on s'aperçoive qu'il *en* parle, et même, tout court, qu'il parle. Ce qui reviendrait, en fait, à conférer au récit biographique et autobiographique, un certain don de ventriloquie.[113]

Calle-Gruber goes on to argue that the autobiographical narrative of the *Nouveau Roman* author "doit rester impossible, c'est-à-dire privée de support unitaire d'énonciation (narrateur, personnage, personnage-narrateur) et, par suite, privée d'*effet biographique* - effet auquel tend peu ou prou tout récit de fiction, lequel est toujours reconductible, dans l'ordre du plus ou moins naturaliste, à l'un de ces trois schémas: ou bien il est *supposé* récit de vie; ou bien il est récit *supposé* de vie (et devient alors reconstitution); ou bien il est récit d'une vie *supposée* (il se donne alors pour invention, mais plausible)."[114]

Robbe-Grillet himself, evidently conscious of this amalgam or mixture of autobiography and fiction, includes in his text a large number of metacommentaries that allude to the ambiguous nature of the text. Approximately the first twenty pages of *Le Miroir qui revient* are, for the most part, metacommentaries on the *Nouveau Roman* and the possibility of writing an autobiographical work faithful to one's past.[115] By beginning his text in this manner, Robbe-Grillet indicates to his reader that he will not be writing a traditional autobiography, but will, while providing insights into his origins, concentrate his efforts on questioning the nature of the autobiographical process. It is via these metacommentaries that Robbe-Grillet explains the choices he has made.[116] He will, for example, attempt to explain the seven-year lapse between the time when he originally started to write his autobiography and the forty-or-so page manuscript that is, in fact, the first forty pages of *Le Miroir qui revient*, which he is now in the process of revising and developing. In a footnote, he also gives the reasons that explain why *Le Miroir qui revient* did not become part of the *Écrivains de toujours* series, published by the Éditions du Seuil:

> J'avais même signé un contrat, toujours valable, avec Paul Flamand. C'est seulement le tour inattendu pris par le texte, au cours de sa composition, qui l'a rendu impropre à figurer dans cette série de petits livres aux dimensions imposées, aux illustrations nombreuses, pour laquelle j'entreprends donc tout autre chose, parallèlement.[10]

It is by means of these self-conscious reflections on the origins and shaping of his work that the reader is introduced to *Le Miroir qui revient* and to the detailed metacommentaries that play a central role in *Romanesques* trilogy. The metacommentaries in *Le Miroir qui revient* set up a frame of reference and prepare the reader for what to expect from this and the other texts in the *Romanesques* series. These detailed metacommentaries fulfill an ideological function, since it is through them that Robbe-Grillet explains or justifies what he is trying to achieve theoretically and politically in his "autofictional narrative." Furthermore, some of these passages have an "emotive" or testimonial function, revealing the author's emotional response towards the story he is recounting. For the most part, these metacommentaries reinforce the function of communication with the reader, especially in those passages where Robbe-Grillet anticipates the questions that the reader would like to ask.

Outside critical judgments have also had an impact on Robbe-Grillet's use of metacommentaries in his work. He is acutely aware of the limited image people have of him. This awareness helps to explain, in part at least, why he finds it necessary to account for and justify the new forms of his "autofictional narratives." Questioned by Michel Rybalka at the Cerisy colloquium in 1971 about the part played by criticism in the elaboration of his works, Robbe-Grillet replied:

> C'est pour moi un apport extrêmement enrichissant, dans la mesure où le critique qui a mis en lumière une signification, dans mes oeuvres, ne m'indique pas une voie à suivre mais une voie à abandonner ... À chaque fois qu'à propos d'un de mes films ou d'un de mes romans j'ai développé moi-même un fragment théorique (quoique je n'aie pas, en général, la tête délibérément théorique, comme peut l'avoir Ricardou), à chaque fois, ce que j'ai eu envie de faire (contre moi, comme j'ai envie de le faire contre les critiques), c'est précisément *autre* chose.[117]

This statement by Robbe-Grillet demonstrates his unwillingness to accept a unified and single interpretation of his work: he writes to destroy ready-made meanings. Moreover, it should be noted that for Robbe-Grillet, as for many of the other *Nouveau Roman* authors, the reception of his writing by the traditional literary critics served as a means for him to understand what was expected of a "true" or traditional novelist. (I place "true" novelist in quotation marks in order to highlight the fact that the work of the *Nouveau Roman* authors was so different from the traditional novel that it overturned the critics' and the readers' conceptions of the novel.) By staging and subverting the conventions of nineteenth-century literature, Robbe-Grillet came to realize his main objective for the *Nouveau Roman* -- creating a new, open and unknowing text that would put meanings into play and meanings into question:

I was reproached, in short, for not being comprehensible, which meant that I, as an author, was supposed to have made clearly understandable that which the character did not understand. And I realized that it was precisely there that a characteristic of newness in modern times occurred, a characteristic which might even be one of the fundamental elements of modernity: things must take place within the text itself.[118]

Investigating the characteristics of the modern novel is so important to Robbe-Grillet that towards the end of *Le Miroir qui revient*, the writer takes up, in a metacommentary, the subject of the sharp dichotomy between the realist novel of the nineteenth century, as characterized by Balzac's work, and the *Nouveau Roman*, of which Flaubert's *Madame Bovary* was the precursor. He explains why in his view, two families of novelists develop along parallel lines:

> En fait, depuis le milieu du dix-neuvième siècle, deux familles de romanciers vont se développer parallèlement. Ceux, d'une part, qui s'obstineront - puisque les valeurs bourgeoises sont toujours en place, à Rome comme à Moscou, même si personne n'y croit plus nulle part - à bâtir des récits codifiés une fois pour toutes selon l'idéologie réaliste sous-balzacienne, sans contradiction ni manque dans la trame signifiante. Et ceux, d'autre part, qui voudront explorer, chaque décennie plus avant, les oppositions insolubles, les éclatements, les apories diégétiques, les cassures, les vides, etc., car ils savent que le réel commence juste au moment où le sens vacille. (213)

Robbe-Grillet presents the *Nouveau Roman* as an active text -- active not only for the reader but for the author as well.[119] It is active because it is an open and incomplete text that puts meaning(s) into question.

To arrive at a clearer idea of Robbe-Grillet's conception of the "autofictional narrative," it is useful to consider his intentions. As there is no shared or general definition of what constitutes an "autofictional narrative," any statement of goals might be helpful in circumscribing the writer's definitions. For example, of stated importance to Robbe-Grillet is the juxtaposition of disparate fragments of memories, myth, history, and theory to expose the multiple facets of a self as both a person and a writer. To a certain extent, Robbe-Grillet considers all of his works autobiographical, as the following statement made during a detailed interview with Jean Monalbetti makes clear:

> Donner un portrait du romancier m'a toujours intéressé. Les romans que j'écrivais dans les années 50 étaient aussi des portraits de moi. Je suis très largement le personnage central de ces romans. Parfois d'ailleurs avec des détails précis. ... Le héros du *Voyeur*, Mathias, a des fantasmes sexuels qui sont très proches des miens. Les écrire à cette époque-là, c'était faire un portrait de moi d'autant plus autobiographique que le décor où Mathias se déplace est celui des landes et falaises où je suis né. Je pense donc que mes livres ont toujours été autobiographiques.[120]

Here, Robbe-Grillet not only speaks to us of his intentions but also clarifies an aspect common to all of his works: the fact that he thinks that all of his books have always been autobiographical. In this critical analysis of his own work, he talks about the continuity between his "novelistic" writing and his "autofictional narratives." Consequently, as is the case for Gide, all the works of Robbe-Grillet may be considered within the flexible limits of the domain of "autobiographical space." These intentions of Robbe-Grillet emphasize the problematic status in his works of fact and fiction, especially for the reader who aspires to distinguish between what really existed in the life of the author, what the author thought existed, and what the author invented. Nonetheless, since Robbe-Grillet mixes fact, fiction, and metacommentaries in the *Romanesques* trilogy, a distinction must be made, from the *reader's* perspective, between these three works and his earlier ones. The earlier works are presented as fictional, whereas the *Romanesques* works obviously include fictional and non-fictional material as the author explicitly points out within the body of the text itself.

To understand better these three hybrid works and how they extend the notion of "autobiographical space," it is helpful to focus on two of their more prominent characteristics. The first characteristic is the blatant, insistent, and self-conscious undermining of the traditional autobiography through the introduction of the fictional character of Henri de Corinthe. The narrative voice that recounts the fictional/historical stories of Corinthe is distinct from the narrative voice that recounts "traditional" childhood memories and from the narrative voice that makes metacommentaries on the autobiographical writing process at the level of *énonciation*. Corinthe plays an essential role since he becomes the alter ego, the double in literature, of Robbe-Grillet himself. In an article on the new autobiographies, Raylene O'Callaghan explains this as follows:

> Robbe-Grillet's first person organizing narrator is accompanied by a legendary third person figure, Henri de Corinthe, fascist and macho or perhaps hero and victim, figure who accedes to a shadowy existence which sets the rational subject against the fantasmatic and the emotional, the logical ordering subject against the disordered and the sexual, the ego against the id. The "I" insisted Roland Barthes, following Lacan, cannot be written except where there is a "representation" of the "imaginaire" ... Robbe-Grillet claims: "J'ai formulé un pacte nouveau. C'est l'imaginaire qui parle; l'imaginaire parle du souvenir."[121]

According to O'Callaghan's theory, Robbe-Grillet succeeds in staging "the imaginary" via the fictional character of Corinthe. Robbe-Grillet is thus able to examine the phantasmic facets of his own personality through the telling of Corinthe's story. The claim that the disordered and sexual subject is set against the logical ordering subject and the id against the ego is useful for an understanding of the mechanisms at work in Robbe-Grillet's texts. Although the *Romanesques* trilogy is different from what Robbe-Grillet had previously written in that they combine autobiographical and fictitious elements with critical theories, they do demonstrate a technique that Robbe-Grillet has always striven to perfect in his books: fragmentation of the narrative voice and of the character's consciousness combined with the continual attempt to put the fragments in order. Robbe-Grillet himself explains:

> For me, the turning point in my work is *Dans le labyrinthe* where, for the first time in my books, there appears a kind of rupture within the narrative word. *Le Voyeur* and *La Jalousie* are, in fact, strongly centered novels which, in the case of *La Jalousie*, means that whether called "husband" or "pure anonymous presence," there is something which is an organizing center of the whole text. This is true of *Le Voyeur* as well. Starting with *Dans le labyrinthe*, however, we have the impression of being in the presence of two distinct voices; without ever knowing which voice we are penetrating, we nevertheless feel, from time to time, their antagonism.[122]

According to Robbe-Grillet himself, in his novels, after and including *Dans le labyrinthe*, there are two potentially antagonistic forces: a narrator and a fragmented character unceasingly in search of the self. In the *Romanesques* trilogy, there is Robbe-Grillet as author and protagonist narrating his past with some invented facts, Robbe-Grillet as theorist who discusses the meanings of his techniques with his readers and there are also the adventures of the fictional character of Corinthe representing Robbe-Grillet's "imaginary."[123] These stories about Corinthe include not only war escapades but fanciful encounters with elusive and seductive females. The mystique of Corinthe is enhanced by the fact that, at the beginning of *Le Miroir qui revient*, he is presented as a friend of Robbe-Grillet's father and as a soldier who periodically makes obscure visits to Robbe-Grillet's childhood home. Although Corinthe is introduced as a "real" person, this character does not have a consistent identity. No reliable dates are given, nor any indications as to his exact whereabouts. In *Angélique ou l'enchantement*, a date, November 20, 1914, is given for Corinthe's search for the brigadier general Simon and the beautiful prisoner Carmina. Nonetheless, Corinthe's age is never revealed and other indications of historical time are contradictory. This leads the reader to have doubts about the verisimilitude of the details of his friendship with Robbe-Grillet's father, since Corinthe would have been

too young to have fought in the same battles as Robbe-Grillet's father during World
War I. Robbe-Grillet himself gives an explanation for this confusion of dates in the
text of *Le Miroir qui revient*:

> Quand j'étais enfant, je croyais que Corinthe était d'abord,
> pour mon père, un camarade de tranchées. Leur amitié, inexplicable
> autrement, ne pouvait être née que dans la boue glorieuse de la Cote
> 108 et des Eparges. J'ai compris bien plus tard que c'était tout à fait
> impossible. Mon père avait vingt ans en 14 et Henri de Corinthe,
> beaucoup plus jeune que lui, n'était certainement pas en âge de
> participer à cette guerre-là, fût-ce comme engagé volontaire à la veille
> de l'armistice. La confusion tenace où je demeurais, sur ce point
> important, provenait sans aucun doute du côté légendaire qu'avait pris
> de façon précoce, dans mon imagination, ce conflit fabuleux, pourtant
> encore tout proche, qu'on appelait simplement "la Grande Guerre"
> comme pour la distinguer à l'avance de toutes les autres, plus
> anciennes ou à venir. (71)

This confusion of dates cautions the reader to always keep in mind that Corinthe is
fundamentally a phantasmic and fictional character. As a result of this confusion of
dates and the fact that Corinthe is presented as a "real" person, there is a constant
movement between truth and fiction, memory and imagination, order and disorder
as Robbe-Grillet questions his memory process and the truth value of Corinthe:

> Qui était Henri de Corinthe? Je pense -- ai-je déjà dit -- ne
> l'avoir jamais rencontré moi-même, sauf, peut-être, lorsque j'étais
> encore un tout petit enfant. Mais les souvenirs personnels qu'il me
> semble parfois avoir gardés de ces brèves entrevues (au sens propre
> du mot: comme entre les deux battants disjoints d'une porte
> accidentellement mal close) ***ont très bien pu avoir été forgés après
> coup par ma mémoire*** - *mensongère et travailleuse - sinon de toutes
> pièces, du moins à partir seulement des récits décousus qui
> circulaient à voix basse dans ma famille, ou aux alentours de la
> vieille maison.* (*Le miroir qui revient*, 7-8, my italics and my
> emphasis)

In order to account for the problematic ontological status of this text in the light of such contradictory and complex movements and memory processes, it is necessary to enlarge Lejeune's narrow definition of the "autobiographical pact" to include not only the identity among the author, the narrator and the protagonist, but also, the imaginary double(s) of protagonist/narrator/author). Analogous in functioning as doubles, though different in status from Robbe-Grillet's fictional character Corinthe, are the three types of narration in Duras' *L'Amant* and the three dialoguing voices in Sarraute's *Enfance*. Duras does not give names to her "alter egos" (i.e., the young Duras as seen by the omniscient narrator and the older Duras as seen by the omniscient narrator); the doubles are indicated simply by *elle* or "she." This technique provides Duras with the means to distance herself from her text. For Sarraute, the voice of the author-narrator trying to remember engages in dialogue with the voice of the alter ego representing the point of view of the adult author. These interruptions of the narrative of childhood memories by the voices of the alter ego are metatextual passages because they make commentaries on what is in the process of being told.

It thus appears that the principal role of the fictional character of Corinthe is to sustain the force of the illusory ego and to subvert the autobiographical narrative. As a reader, one finds, for example, that the uncertainties about Corinthe's past parallel the uncertainties that Robbe-Grillet has about his own past. By illustrating the difficulties encountered in trying to accurately relate Corinthe's past, using only sketchy and fragmented family stories as sources of information, Robbe-Grillet succeeds in demonstrating to the reader the uneasiness he experiences in writing about his own childhood since he is dependent upon family stories for many of the details. In *Le Miroir qui revient*, Robbe-Grillet stresses the difference between an experience remembered directly and one brought back through stories: "J'ai retrouvé alors, inchangée, l'impression affreuse de jadis et j'ai pensé que le pauvre moineau écrasé devait être un vrai souvenir et *non pas, comme souvent, une histoire que mes parent m'auraient racontée ensuite.*" (202, my italics)   In fact, Robbe-Grillet continually questions the validity not only of his memories from his own past but also of those from Corinthe's past:

> Henri de Corinthe, son souvenir du moins, m'apparaît (m'est toujours apparu?) comme plus fuyant encore, plus insaisissable, et souvent même suspect, pour ne pas dire plus. Était-il un imposteur, lui aussi, bien que d'un tout autre genre? Beaucoup de ceux qui l'ont connu le pensent aujourd'hui, à plus forte raison ceux dont les informations et images sont puisées dans la seule presse à scandales. (70)

Corinthe's role becomes much more complex and his character is more clearly linked to the present writing process in *Angélique ou l'enchantement*. In *Le Miroir qui revient*, Corinthe makes only seven intermittent appearances, whereas, in *Angélique ou l'enchantement*, thirty of the sixty-five "chapters"[124] are either dedicated solely to the adventures of Corinthe or are reflections made on this fictional character. For example, Robbe-Grillet talks about his attempts, in Buenos Aires, to trace Corinthe's path after the latter's dramatic departure from Uruguay in the weeks following the mysterious disappearance of his fiancée, Marie-Ange (131-134). Writing on the subsequent development of Corinthe, Sheringham comments:

> The main strategy is to augment the fictional dimension, but also to alter its alignment with the other material, creating a topology in which the text's various surfaces are never securely mapped. *Angélique* is not focused on the origins of the writer's activities but on the activity of writing itself and its relation to fantasy, particulary the sado-erotic fantasies Robbe-Grillet seems anxious to come clean about.[125]

In demonstrating the complexities of the autobiographical writing process, Robbe-Grillet presents Corinthe as an autobiographical writer (albeit of a missing text). He may thus be viewed as a mouthpiece for perverse or ironic renderings of Robbe-

Grillet's ideas. Robbe-Grillet's first description of Corinthe's work suggests the singularity of the latter:

> Je suis en train de m'égarer. C'est de Corinthe qu'il devrait s'agir (non de moi) et, en premier lieu, de ce que nous pouvons encore rassembler aujourd'hui comme témoignages concernant l'impact ou le développement de ses singulières idées, avant, pendant et après la guerre. Si le manuscrit du grand livre qu'il rédigeait n'avait pas été détruit, dont nous supposons seulement qu'il contenait un mélange -- mouvant lui aussi -- d'autobiographie et de théorie "révolutionnaire", auquel s'ajoutait (du moins je le soupçonne) une part indéterminée de politique-fiction, pour ne pas dire de roman, nous en saurions certes davantage sur ce sujet comme sur beaucoup d'autres.[126]

Two first-person narrative subjects will consequently develop as Robbe-Grillet switches, without any transitional remarks, in the middle of his third-person narrative about Corinthe to the use of first-person narration. Corinthe is allowed to speak directly for himself through first-person narration. In the following example, there is a dramatic switch in narrative voice as the first-person narrating subject changes from Robbe-Grillet to Corinthe by the insertion of the use of *moi*:

> Avec lenteur, l'inconnu relève enfin ses grands yeux clairs en direction du capitaine français qui vient d'apparaître, interrompant comme à regret sa méditation. Puis, dans un large mouvement souple et régulier d'une perfection d'épure, qui paraît avoir été tourné au ralenti, il dégaine son sabre pour en présenter le métal nu verticalement devant son visage, menton levé, le tranchant de l'acier exposé face à *moi*, le dos non coupant de la lame effleurant presque sa bouche et son nez, en un cérémonieux salut de parade. (138, my italics)

The fictional character of Corinthe now represents a multiplication and a displacement of the traditional narrative voice as he intermittently interrupts the autobiographical narrative.[127] There are also examples of when switches in narrative voice are not so readily apparent to the reader:

> Le comte Henri a dû quitter sa table de travail pour observer
> le temps qu'il fait au dehors, (...) Puis il se retourne en direction des
> papiers répandus sur toute la superficie de la grande table en noyer,
> (...) qui constituent les multiples brouillons successifs du manuscrit
> auquel il consacre depuis plusieurs années la majeure partie de ses
> loisirs, et dont un célèbre éditeur parisien fera disparaître l'unique
> exemplaire final dans des conditions encore aujourd'hui (ainsi que *je*
> l'ai déjà signalé dans le premier tome de ce mémoire), ... (12, my
> italics)

Here, the reader is presented with the image of Corinthe working on his manuscripts

at his black table. This passage is told in third-person narration with only one

intrusion, in the form of a parenthetical remark, by Robbe-Grillet as narrator who

makes an intertextual reference to *Le Miroir qui revient* ("le premier tome de ce

mémoire"). Then in the next paragraph, there is a switch in narration from third- to

first-person as is indicated by the possessive noun marker *mon*:

> Au-delà du bureau ainsi garni de feuilles en désordre qui
> forment par endroit un épais tapis, se dresse l'armoire à glace où se
> reflète *mon* image, si peu distincte dans la pénombre qu'il m'a semblé
> d'abord découvrir à l'autre bout de la pièce un étranger, qui se serait
> introduit là sans bruit tandis que j'avais le dos tourné vers la fenêtre.
> (13, my italics)

The confusion in this narrative slippage is brought about by the fact that the narrator

is working at a desk covered with papers -- which is a situation very similar to the

one describing Corinthe in the previous paragraph. When, in addition, the narrator

is disturbed when he discovers the perplexing image of an *étranger* behind his own

image, his befuddlement creates an unstable narrative situation. The reader is thus

initially left uncertain as to whether it is Robbe-Grillet the narrator looking at

Corinthe's image reflected in the mirror or, if it is Corinthe the narrator looking at

Robbe-Grillet's, or a completely different person's, image reflected in the mirror or

whether all of this is a figment of one or the other's imagination. As a result of this

constant splitting of the narrator's role, the reader must grapple with the complexity of the narrative situation. Calle-Gruber maintains: "La mobilité des pronoms et des figures auxquelles ils renvoient, fait du sujet non plus une énigme de la personne mais un paradigme de personnages dont les virtualités sont infinies: je est, dans ce dispositif, incessamment *substituable*; je est toujours substitut."[128] In fact, by changing the narrative of Corinthe from third- to first-person, Robbe-Grillet reinforces the reader's impression that Corinthe is not a fictional character but a "real" person. But more importantly, the double first-person narrative allows for parallels to be drawn between Robbe-Grillet and his mythical alter ego. In an article entitled "Un miroir enchanté," Sjef Houppermans writes of the double "je" in *Angélique ou l'enchantement*:

> Pour le "je" la notion de double s'intensifie dans une bipartite présence poursuivie de Corinthe: d'abord comme l'autre auteur -- lui aussi écrit des mémoires dont les limites restent incertaines; mais à travers ce personnage en/de lettres insiste et persiste son *image*, image dans le miroir, image cherchée dans les portraits, image projetée sur la route, image finalement et spécifiquement réintroduite dans le roman des origines qui constitue-décompose les origines des "romanesques".[129]

For Calle-Gruber, "*Je* assume la prise de parole mais pour n'être plus que *porte* parole de tous les parleurs convoqués, médiateur des récits et lectures retransmis."[130] For Sheringham, in contrast to Calle-Gruber who interprets the double *je* in terms of its linguistic functions, "the device suggests that to write is to become someone else, to try on identities which our fantasies construct for us."[131] One could maintain that Robbe-Grillet uses the character of Corinthe as a means of analyzing various "ghosts" from his past and examining the difficulties of their translation in the writing process. In *Le Miroir qui revient*, for example, Robbe-Grillet writes of the childhood nightmares that were brought about by his still unconquered fear of the sea. The moment he lost consciousness, the sea would dominate his thoughts and cause him to wake up screaming. Even his mother's remedy of linctus of bromide did not cure his terrible nightmares. The reader may wonder whether Robbe-Grillet recounts the story of Corinthe's discovery of the mirror that bore the haunting image of Marie-Ange, his dead fiancée, as a way of consciously examining his own nightmares. Corinthe had found the mirror floating in the sea and, after seeing the image of Marie-Ange reflected in it, lost consciousness. A coastguard revives Corinthe whose subsequent behavior becomes incomprehensible. One could also maintain that Robbe-Grillet uses the fictional character of Corinthe as a means of coming to terms with his sado-erotic fantasies. In *Angélique ou l'enchantement*, the erotic imagination of the young Robbe-Grillet is at the forefront of the narrative, reinforced by the adult reflections on the role played by sadism and sexual crime in male fantasy. Throughout the narrative, Robbe-Grillet writes about Henri de Corinthe's adventures in the enchanted forest with the *belle captive* or "beautiful prisoner" who is not simply a victim but a bewitching sorceress who lures men into her traps. At the very end of *Angélique ou l'enchantement*, the reader is presented with stories of Robbe-Grillet's childhood playmate, Angélique Arno. Angélique, who was twelve, would tease the thirteen year-old Robbe-Grillet in a variety of ways in order to arouse his sexual curiosity. The reader is led to draw parallels between the stories about Corinthe in the enchanted forest and the young Robbe-Grillet. In *Les Derniers jours de Corinthe*, the narrator explains how he continues to be powerless against the narrative of Corinthe:

> On a vu, j'espère, quelques lignes plus haut, comment nous avons évité de justesse le retour in opiné du lecteur surpris vers la forêt enchantée de Perte-lès-Hurles, quelque part entre Verdun et les Ardennes, en ce mois de novembre 1914 dont il a été longuement question dans le précédent volume de mon rapport. Mais voilà que revient malgré tout le comte Henri, plus obstiné que moi encore, à la faveur de cet aparté inutilement ironique du narrateur.[132]

In addition, in *Les Derniers jours de Corinthe*, Corinthe, speaking for himself through first-person narration, makes a direct reference to Robbe-Grillet as a writer, further enhancing the illusion that Corinthe is a real person.[133] Moreover, as Robbe-Grillet warns the reader in *Angélique ou l'enchantement* about the forthcoming dense theoretical section, he warns the reader about the hallucinatory narrative about Corinthe to follow in *Les Derniers jours de Corinthe*:

> Quant au texte qui suit, là où les feuilles clairement rédigées prennent à nouveau le relais des brouillons couverts de ratures, de contradictions et de ressassements, il apparaît surtout comme le fruit maladif d'hallucinations colorées, presque abstraites, qui peuvent n'avoir qu'un lointain rapport avec la réalité objective, chère (en théorie du moins) à notre auteur, faisant plutôt songer aux toiles du peintre Paoli, que l'on ne doit pas confondre avec un autre artiste moins connu nommé Yves Simon, lequel est en même temps poète et chirurgien. (161)

Thus, the stories about Corinthe serve as a further way for Robbe-Grillet to explore his fantasies. Moreover, Corinthe's death prevents Robbe-Grillet from finishing his memoir. He concludes *Les Derniers jours de Corinthe* by stating: "Le moment est donc venu. Selon ce qui a été prescrit, je signe ici mon mémoire in achevé (229)," and consequently symbolically demonstrates to the reader the inability to write a complete and accurate autobiography. The stories about Corinthe serve as a further way for Robbe-Grillet to explore his fantasies.

The second noteworthy characteristic of the *Romanesques* trilogy is the constant and intrusive metacommentaries that Robbe-Grillet makes on the problematic nature of his texts. They are considered by many critics as excessive (Robbe-Grillet includes metacommentaries in his autobiographical text to a *much greater* extent than either Sarraute or Duras), self-indulgent, and irritating for the reader who must juggle many frames of reference because of the abrupt transitions in the narrative. The metacommentaries are so extensive that a different kind of text is set up for the reader. In fact, these sudden changes in the text through the metacommentaries are felt by the reader as an infraction of the point of view previously established by the context. This is especially apparent when Robbe-Grillet breaks the flow of the narrative of his past or that of the fictional character of Henri de Corinthe to introduce a didactic metacommentary in order to explain or justify his position. This may give some readers the impression that he is a manipulative author, whereas others may rationalize that these metacommentaries are part of the writer's life since he has dedicated it to the understanding and improvement of the novel and that, as such, they should be included in his "autofictional narrative." Robbe-Grillet will, for example, repeatedly refer to the sensory underpinnings of the creative writing process: "Aujourd'hui comme alors, cependant, je n'écris jamais rien sans le voir dans mes yeux de façon quasiment matérielle." (*Angélique ou l'enchantement* 10) The reader is thus exposed to metacommentaries that continually focus on the way his writing develops. At the very beginning of *Le Miroir qui revient*, he proposes a possible answer to the question of why he struggles to render the memories of his past:

> Ce n'est probablement que dans le but -- incertain -- de donner à de telles questions ne serait-ce *qu'un semblant de réponse, que j'ai entrepris, il y a quelque temps déjà, de rédiger cette autobiographie.* Et voilà que, me mettant à en relire les premières pages, après un laps fatidique de sept ans, c'est à peine si j'y reconnais les choses dont je voulais parler de toute urgence. Ainsi en va-t-il de l'écriture: à la fois recherche solitaire, têtue, presque intemporelle, et soumission moqueuse aux préoccupations du moment, "mondaines" en quelque sorte. (9, my italics)

This metacommentary hints at what governs Robbe-Grillet's project -- at once the immediate questions of the self and the solitary, persistant research on the writing process -- thereby providing insights as well for the reader. In the following passage, a continuation of the previous metacommentary, Robbe-Grillet defends his writing and his intention of persisting in going against the representational norms of the "true" or traditional novelist:

> En ce début des années 80, la réaction est soudainement redevenue si forte contre toute tentative d'échapper aux normes de l'expression-représentation traditionnelle, que mes imprudentes remarques de naguère, au lieu de jouer leur rôle décapant contre un dogme nouveau qui commençait alors à s'introduire (l'anti-humanisme), n'ont plus l'air aujourd'hui que de glisser sur la pente savonneuse du discours dominant restauré, l'éternel bon vieux discours de jadis que j'avais au départ si ardemment combattu. Dans la vague de "retour à" qui déferle sur nous de toute part, on risque fort de ne plus voir que j'espérais au contraire un dépassement, une "relève". (9)

Here, Robbe-Grillet evokes the conservative reaction of the nineteen eighties and the danger that his own revolutionary discourse may simply be assimilated to the dominant discourse. This leads him to develop, in an extended metaphorical metacommentary, an image of the danger of theories going stale and becoming dogma:

> L'idéologie, toujours masquée, change facilement de figure. C'est une hydre-miroir, dont la tête coupée reparaît bien vite à neuf, présentant à l'adversaire son propre visage, qui se croyait vainqueur. (11)

Through this visual image of ideology as a hydra-mirror, that is, a many-headed monster that self regenerates, the reader is better able to associate with the author's difficulties in destroying or upsetting established theoretical dogmas.

The reader of the *Romanesques* trilogy is also confronted with many metacommentaries referring to Robbe-Grillet's previous writings and to the writings of other authors that influenced his work. Metacommentaries on intertextual references to his previous writings range once again from justifications of his writing practices to incidental information related to the genesis of a particular work. For example, in *Le Miroir qui revient* (35) he writes of the first time he saw a German soldier during the Occupation and of how this incident became the source of inspiration for *Dans le labyrinthe*. Or for example, in *Le Miroir qui revient*, he comments on how he had not yet solved the problem of "expression" and the excessive use of metaphor in *Le Régicide*, his first attempt at a novel. He then remarks on the influence of Camus' *L'Étranger* and Sartre's *La Nausée*:

> Le plus visible des conflits internes qui organisent la structure de ce récit [*Le Régicide*] est précisément l'opposition stylistique entre le constat et l'expression, c'est-à-dire entre l'écriture "neutre" et le recours systématique aux charmes pompeux de la métaphore. Déjà sous cet angle, la figure centrale du texte -- Boris, conscience narratrice unique et fortement personnalisée, qui s'exprime même la moitié du temps à la première personne -- s'inscrit dans la famille illustrée, lors de la décennie précédante, par le Meursault de Camus et le Roquentin de Sartre. (164)

He then continues by explaining how the influence of Camus and Sartre resulted in shaping the direction his work was to take.[134] It is thus via both the intertextual references to his other works and the references to the works of other authors that Robbe-Grillet is able to talk about the way his work was shaped by other writing and to define himself. However, as is always the case with intertextual references and references to other authors' works, the reader must be familiar with these outside works in order to follow the author's line of thinking. It seems that a principal function of these metacommentaries is to set up a text different from that of the traditional autobiographical narrative by giving so much focus to aesthetic theory and ideology. Thus the text becomes what Calle-Gruber would term *autographie*: "Je nomme ainsi le dispositif qui consiste à déplacer les enjeux, du personnage vers le narrateur, de la scène des représentations vers la mise en spectacle, de la référence au monde vers la référence aux textes -- tous les textes précédemment écrits par le signataire, eux-mêmes porteurs d'autres textes."[135]

Conscious of the preeminence of the adult author's point of view in an autobiography, Robbe-Grillet seeks to share a sustained reflection on point of view with the reader -- once again through the use of metacommentaries. The dimension of the temporal gap between the event and its notation is very important for the definition of autobiography as well as for that of "autobiographical space" because in an autobiography, the choice of memories implies not only the work's central principle but also the preeminence of the point of view of the adult author. In *Le Miroir qui revient*, Robbe-Grillet's metacommentary concentrates on his own uncertainties about the nature of the important and difficult process of selecting memories:

> Une fois de plus je me demande à quoi riment ces évocations. Pourquoi raconter ainsi longuement ces petites anecdotes plus ou moins vaines. Si elles m'apparaissent un tant soit peu significatives, je me reproche aussitôt de les avoir choisies (arrangées, confectionnées peut-être) précisément pour signifier. Si au contraire ce ne sont que des fragments perdus, à la dérive, pour lesquels je serais moi-même à la recherche d'un sens possible, quelle raison a pu me faire isoler seulement ceux-là, parmi les centaines, les milliers qui se présentent en désordre. (56)

The questioning of the nature of the choice of memories not only evokes the problematic nature of the principle central to autobiography but also suggests the dangers inherent in this choice. In an article on the conditions and limits of autobiography, Georges Gusdorf writes: "Le péché originel de l'autobiographie est donc d'abord celui de cohérence logique et de rationalisation. Le récit est conscience, et comme la conscience du narrateur mène le récit, il lui paraît invinciblement qu'elle a mené sa vie. ... Pareillement l'autobiographie est condamnée à substituer sans cesse le tout fait au se faisant. Le présent vécu, avec sa charge d'insécurité, se trouve pris dans le mouvement nécessaire qui relie, au fil du récit, le passé à l'avenir."[136] It is impossible for an autobiography to entirely avoid this type of simplification "de substituer le tout fait au se faisant" because the autobiographer has no choice but to look at the past from his current vantage point. It is necessary to pay attention, as Robbe-Grillet strives to do, to the danger of distortion. He explains this in a metacommentary that echoes the theories of Gusdorf:

C'est un autre problème qui se pose, du fait que je parle aussi de moi; ou même: uniquement de moi, comme toujours. Mes parents, c'est déjà moi en train de prendre forme. *À qui veut l'entendre, j'affirme récuser l'entreprise autobiographique, où l'on prétend rassembler toute une existence vécue (qui, dans l'instant, faisait eau de toute part) en un volume clos, sans manques et sans bavures*, comme font ces vieux maréchaux qui remettent dans une ordonnance convaincante, pour les générations futures, leurs anciennes batailles mal gagnées, ou perdues. *Or je me sens, à tout moment, menacé par cette pente, par ce précipice que je côtoie. Il ne suffit pas d'en percevoir les dangers pour échapper à sa fascination.* (*Le Miroir qui revient* 58, my italics)

In this critical observation, Robbe-Grillet expresses his opposition to the claims of traditional autobiographers who have put the whole of a life together but he also recognizes that he too would find it easy to fall into this trap. The problem that Robbe-Grillet highlights here could find an explanation in Roy Pascal's argument: "in the face of the great richness of modern autobiography in so far as it tells of the development of a specific gift and task, its success in representing the whole man is relatively meagre. I do not think this is due to the technical difficulty of combining many threads in a story; it arises above all from a certain falling short in respect of the whole personality."[137] Robbe-Grillet's attention to the danger of distortion imposed by the adult point of view is also demonstrated by the continual references to the possibility that he may have invented certain memories based upon stories that his family told him. His suspicion of the processes of memory and uncertainty about his own memory process and detailed recollection of past events further motivate the metacommentaries that directly analyze his memory process. Robbe-Grillet's method of questioning his memory process is similar to Sarraute's technique of the dialogic exchange between the voice of the author-narrator trying to remember and the voice of the alter ego who scrutinizes and verifies what the other voice has recounted. The difference between these two authors' techniques is that Sarraute will use direct discourse between the two voices in a subtle form of metacommentary whereas Robbe-Grillet will directly address his narratee and eventual reader. Robbe-Grillet, in addressing his narratee and eventual reader directly in his numerous metacommentaries, has developed an effective, though somewhat wearisome for some readers, way of showing the doubts that he has as an autobiographer. For example, in *Le Miroir qui revient*, remarking on a memory of a meeting between Corinthe and his father, he writes:

> *Le passage qui précède doit être entièrement inventé.* La maison de famille était modeste, relativement grande et protégée par quelques arbres, mais bâtie en torchis, la marine militaire interdisant les constructions à caractère définitif dans cette zone qui dépendait alors du port de guerre. *Pourtant les chocs sourds et répétés qui ébranlent le sol de granit appartiennent sans aucun doute à mes impressions d'enfance.* (24, my italics)

Even though Robbe-Grillet makes clear to his reader his doubts about the autobiographical memory process, in *Le Miroir qui revient*, he does make an exception by mentioning a very powerful and haunting personal recollection. This memory is particulary poignant for him because of a recent event that triggered the involuntary memory process of this particular past event. The memory concerns the young Robbe-Grillet's anguish at having crushed a baby sparrow with his foot in order to put it out of its misery. The bird was badly injured and was dragging itself round in circles on his elementary school playground. The young boy feels extremely guilty for he knows that his mother would have tried to save the bird's life. This memory is related to a strange sensation, a mixture of horror and fascination. What brought this particular incident back to mind was the recent deliberate squashing of a young coypu or muskrat:

> Le mois dernier, près de l'embarcadère de la pièce d'eau inférieure, au Mesnil, j'ai volontairement foulé sous ma botte un bébé ragondin (on devrait dire plus exactement, je crois, rat musqué ou ondatra). Ces gros rongeurs aquatiques et terricoles pullulent en Normandie depuis la guerre, des élevages ayant été libérés dans la nature par les combats, prétend-on, et Catherine se fait du souci

quand ils prolifèrent au sein des berges, don't ils minent les profondeurs au point d'en ruiner la résistance et d'abattre les arbres entre les racines desquels ils ont établi leurs logements aux multiples galeries. *J'ai retrouvé alors, inchangée, l'impression affreuse de jadis et j'ai pensé que le pauvre moineau écrasé devait être un vrai souvenir et non pas, comme souvent, une histoire que mes parents m'auraient racontée ensuite.* (201-202, my italics)

It is through the incident of the crushed coypu that the memory of the crushed sparrow is triggered. As for Sarraute, sensation is the touchstone for the truth or reality of the memory. Robbe-Grillet feels confident in his remembering of this guilt-laden incident from his childhood, since he is not relying on one of his parents' stories but on the capacity of his own affective memory. By giving us a detailed account of the memory process based on analogous sensory impressions, the writer suggests to himself and to his reader that it is possible, through one's own means, to be reasonably certain of the veracity of a childhood memory.

A second, yet different, example in *Le Miroir qui revient* of when Robbe-Grillet is sure of the accuracy of the process of remembrance is the vivid recollection triggered by a word phrase used by his father. His father, who had suffered an injury to the head during World War One and who appeared not to be bothered by it in the least, would readily admit: "J'ai l'impression d'avoir des marchandises mal arrimées dans le crâne..." (83) This phrase reminds Robbe-Grillet of how for years his father attempted to be officially recognized as insane in order to supplement his military pension. This word phrase also brings to Robbe-Grillet's mind another expression used by his family in reference to mental unease:

> Ses marchandises mal arrimées me rappellent une autre formule qui avait cours chez nous pour signifier un certain type d'angoisse, ou de malaise mental profond: "j'ai des raies dans la tête," "cette histoire me donne des raies dans la tête" ... L'expression provenait d'un conte de Kipling, *Le Perturbateur de trafic*, dans lequel un gardien devient fou tout en haut de son phare, perdu au milieu des eaux dangereuses entre les îles de la Sonde. (84)

Robbe-Grillet demonstrates, as Sarraute does, how a particular word phrase helps to strengthen the lasting effect of a memory. The word phrases, which are reproduced directly in the narrative discourse, have lingered on in the author's memory because they made a profound impression on him when he was a child and because the memory process is based upon metonymic associations. What is important here is that the expression or the text as it is read plays a vital role in the memory of the past and that we are never outside language.

Although one might assume that the reader is already familiar with Robbe-Grillet's literary practice and might not be in need of further didactic metacommentaries after having read *Le Miroir qui revient*, their use, as was previously stated, is much more extensive in *Angélique ou l'enchantement*, the second book in the *Romanesques* series. In fact, a major portion of the book -- to be more exact, pages 158 to 215 -- is pure theory. However, in the pages preceding this polemical section, there is a patchwork of various kinds of writing that take the reader far beyond the autobiographical narrative. There is a full range of heterogeneous elements that make up what Robbe-Grillet himself refers to as his *autobiographie fantasmée* or "phantasmic autobiography"[138]: elaborate details of his sexual fantasies, extensive use of the *romans de chevalerie* or "chivalric romances" based on the adventures of his father and of Corinthe, Breton legends, ghost stories, and passages where he tries to remember events from his past that contrast with the passages that are imaginary take-offs from images and photos.[139] In fact, the paratextual information on the back cover of *Angélique ou l'enchantement* only begins to prepare the reader for the full range of heterogeneous elements that are found between the covers of this intriguing text:

> Ce second volume des *Romanesques* de Robbe-Grillet fait, dans une certaine mesure, suite au *Miroir qui revient*. ... Mais, cette fois, ce sont surtout les imaginations érotiques du petit garçon qui occupent le devant de la scène, en même temps que les réflexions de l'adulte sur le rôle joué par le sadisme et le crime sexuel dans la

fantasmatique masculine. ... Ainsi la Grande Guerre quitte son visage de boue pour se dérouler à présent dans une sorte de forêt enchantée, où dragons français et uhlans prussiens sont aux prises avec des fées-fleurs aux troublants sortilèges, dont on est en droit de se demander si elles ne sont pas tout autre chose que des jeunes espionnes suscitées par l'ennemi.

The reader is immediately alerted to the fanciful and heterogeneous stories that are the substance of the second volume of this "phantasmic autobiography." Particularly striking is the story told about his father riding alone in a fairy-tale landscape:

Cavalier solitaire, il s'avance le long d'une route plate et rectiligne, mal empierrée, assez étroite, bordée çà et là de jeunes peupliers mutilés par les récents combats, dont les branches sans feuillage, éclatées et pendantes, émergent soudain en gris plus sombre au milieu d'un épais brouillard, dans la clarté funèbre de la nuit. (41)

Continuing this story of his father's adventure in an enchanted forest that has a hazy aura of spells and charms, Robbe-Grillet introduces a mysterious old man:

Une voix lente, grave, très lasse, se fait entendre enfin, donnant la troublante impression qu'elle émane du brouillard même, flottante et diffuse comme lui. (...) "C'est moi qui te salue, dit-il, beau soldat!" La formule cérémonieuse, archaïque, peu habituelle en tout cas, est rendue plus remarquable encore par une pause trop marquée (...) Afin de secouer la gêne qui l'envahit, mon père demande: "C'est votre charrette, peut-être, dont on entend les grincements là-bas, devant nous?" Et sa propre phrase le surprend, au moment même où il la prononce, par son tour guindé, sa prosodie pompeuse, son manque de naturel. (43)

Also recounted in a style reminiscent of fairy tales and legends are the chimerical stories about Corinthe. For example, Corinthe's search for the brigadier general Simon and the beautiful prisoner Carmina, is interrupted by his meeting up with Manrica, an enigmatic seductress:

> Elle a l'air d'un petit animal sauvage surpris dans son nid.
> Mais on peut croire au contraire qu'elle vient de se mordre la bouche,
> tout exprès, pour accroître encore un pouvoir de séduction dont elle
> connaît déjà tous les ressorts. Lui rendant son sourire, à tout hasard,
> pour ne pas effrayer l'apparition dans le cas où elle serait malgré tout
> craintive, Corinthe demande: "C'est toi qui chantais?" – "Si ce n'était
> pas une fauvette," répond-elle sans se troubler, "ça devait en effet être
> moi, puisqu'il n'y a personne d'autre!" (94)

The reader, who has adjusted to the interweaving of all the heterogeneous elements
in the text -- including fairy tales and legends -- is taken aback by the abrupt change
in focus and discourse when Robbe-Grillet switches from being an innovative
"autofictional" narrator to being a theoretician who explains why and how he writes
in an attempt to explain the reasons why he has been misunderstood. He is, in effect,
once again justifying his work and appears to be defending himself against criticism.
Consequently, this theoretical section of *Angélique ou l'enchantement* gives the
reader the impression that Robbe-Grillet is no longer writing his autobiography but
his confessions, a kind of "autorhetoric" or "apologia."[140] For example, defending
himself in the face of the many feminist attacks, he writes:

> Enfin je vois mal, quant à moi, comment l'on pourrait
> m'accuser d'avoir dénié aux jeunes femmes le privilège de briller ou
> de s'affirmer sur d'autres plans, et d'une tout autre manière. L'héroïne
> en particulier de mon roman le plus connu, le plus lu aujourd'hui, le
> plus étudié à travers le monde, *La Jalousie*, serait là pour témoigner
> du contraire. (160)

These metacommentaries may prove to be too heavyhanded, polemical, and intrusive
for the reader, giving one the feeling of being in a totally different book. This is
especially true of Robbe-Grillet's metacommentaries that are counterattacks against
feminist readings. In fact, these metacommentaries give the reader the impression
that the author is giving a lecture rather than recounting his past. For example, he
gives a metacommentary on the readability of his work that is reminiscent of the

comments he made in 1982 at the colloquium at New York University on the *Nouveau Roman*:

> Pour reprendre cette terminologie commode, je dirais que mes romans ou mes films -- comme toute oeuvre nouvelle à son surgissement -- apportaient trop d'information aux critiques académiques et à leurs fidèles, ce qui les rendait à la lettre incompréhensibles. ... *Mes romans n'étaient pas "lisibles"* (ils le deviennent ensuite peu à peu), mais les essais critiques de *Pour un nouveau roman* le seront de façon immédiate, puisque tout lecteur y distinguait sans mal "les oripeaux de l'ordre ancien", dont on leur faisait voir à présent la doublure. Certes, il la jugeait choquante, mais il en percevait très bien l'agencement. (168-169, my italics)

Possibly the most important metacommentary in all of *Angélique ou l'enchantement* is the one made towards the beginning of the text because it addresses questions of autobiographical writing and develops into an attack on the theories of Lejeune, in particular the latter's definition of the "autobiographical pact":

> Il en irait donc pour les événements de notre passé comme pour ceux du présent: les arrêter n'est pas possible. Instants fragiles, aussi soudainement apparus que vite effacés, nous ne pouvons ni les tenir immobiles, ni en fixer la trace de façon définitive, ni les réunir en une durée continue au sein d'organisations causales à sens unique et sans faille. Ainsi ne saurais-je partager l'avis de Philippe Lejeune concernant la mise en texte des souvenirs. "L'exigence de signification est le principe positif et premier, dit-il, de la quête autobiographique." Non, non! Certainement pas! Cet axiome n'est valable, de toute évidence, ni pour le manuscrit dont la rédaction a occupé Corinthe pendant les deux dernières décennies de son existence, ni pour ma propre entreprise actuelle. (67)

This metacommentary is questioning the demand for meaning as central to the autobiographical project. Robbe-Grillet then continues by giving the reasons why he does not find any differences between his work as a novelist and that as an autobiographer. For him, the assemblage of past events is not at all an attempt to understand one's life history but the means by which to produce new narratives with reference to the past:

> La patiente écriture des fragments qui demeurent (provisoirement, je le sais) ne peut en aucun cas considérer mon passé comme producteur de significations (un sens à ma vie), mais au contraire comme producteur de récit: un devenir à mon projet d'écrivain. (68)

Robbe-Grillet finds it important to point out to his reader that he believes that both autobiography and fiction are narratives that attempt to enable an author to define and describe the self, even though he also believes that the enterprise is an impossible one. Since this attack of Lejeune's theory is based on the latter's definition of the "autobiographical pact," the reader is led to wonder if Robbe-Grillet is aware of, or would still be unhappy with, Lejeune's redefinition and more comprehensive view of autobiographical writing as put forth in the chapter on Gide, where he introduces the broader concept of "autobiographical space." Houppermans reflects on these two metacommentaries by Robbe-Grillet as follows: "l'écriture joue dangereusement sur la frontière entre souvenir et fiction, et ainsi elle introduit d'autres figures dans le sujet, montrant que le moi est une projection de doubles. Et c'est cette autre fiction qui permet au 'je' de retrouver sa liberté, celle d'inventer."[141] These two metacommentaries help the reader to understand why metacommentaries are used so extensively in the "Romanesque" series: Robbe-Grillet feels the need to defend his process of "writing the self" and producing a more open-ended kind of "autofictional narrative." After reading the *Romanesques* trilogy, all rereadings and future new readings of Robbe-Grillet's other works will be affected by the comprehensive metacritical information found in the "Romanesque" texts.

In addition to the two preceding metacommentaries where Robbe-Grillet maintains that both autobiography and fiction are narratives that help to define the self, he indicates, as a response to his own attack on Lejeune's theories, his position on the importance of the structure, rather than the meaning, of a narrative:

> Quant aux organisations des récits dans un cas (les prétendues fictions) comme dans l'autre (les pseudo-recherches autobiographiques), je reconnais sans mal qu'elles représentent le même espoir, sous des formes diverses, de mettre en jeu les deux mêmes questions impossibles -- qu'est-ce que c'est, moi? Et qu'est-ce que je fais là? -- qui ne sont pas des problèmes de signification, mais bel et bien des problèmes de structure. Il ne s'agit donc pas de me rassurer par de fausses cohérences figées, plaquées de l'extérieur. Je dois prendre garde au contraire de toujours ménager le mouvement, les manques, et la contingence inexplicable du vivant. (69)

For Robbe-Grillet, narrative is structure, a moving, contingent, complex structure made up of many heterogeneous elements. A parallel can be drawn between this metacommentary and Robbe-Grillet's comment in the previously mentioned detailed interview with Jean Montalbetti where he maintains that he thinks that all of his works have been autobiographical since many voices can be used to relate a narrative. Here, however, he maintains that the questions central to both so-called "fictional works" and "autofictional narratives" are essentially questions of structure. Both, as he pointed out in a detailed interview with Jacques Henric, are works in movement; his characters, just as he himself, are not stable entities but "effets de personnages."[142]

To guide the reader in following the combination of these many different elements, Robbe-Grillet, in the *Romanesques* trilogy, includes a key piece of paratextual information: it is the *table des matières*, found at the end of all three texts. What is striking is that it is much more than the usual "table of contents": it is a detailed summary of all the heterogeneous elements. The table appears more as an index, since it is not merely a listing of chapter titles but a detailed account of what is discussed in each "chapter." These "chapters" are made up of narrative or metatextual segments or fragments and the separation between each "chapter" is indicated within the body of the text by the skipping of a space. The table takes into consideration the fragmentary nature of each "chapter" by listing the various elements -- narrative and/or metatextual -- in separate paragraphs. A telling example is the following entry from *Angélique ou l'enchantement*:

> Tom protecteur. Ma poupée de chiffon. Je voulais voir M. de Corinthe. L'interdit par le père. Bruit de ses pas. Je m'endors avec ma poupée docile. ... 30. (249)

Striking here are not only the details given but also the abrupt changes in time, place and circumstance from one narrative segment to the next. According to Genette: "À vrai dire, l'usage classique était plutôt de placer en tête une table des chapitres, et à la fin une table des matières proprement dite, sorte d'index plus détaillé. Notre table moderne est en fait une table des chapitres, et son nom est un peu usurpé."[143] Robbe-Grillet's use of the *table des matières* follows its classic definition. Moreover, Robbe-Grillet encourages the use of the table. For example, he suggests to his reader at the beginning of the long theoretical section in *Angélique ou l'enchantement*, that those in a hurry and only interested in the narrative of Corinthe would do better to skip the section that follows and refer to the *table des matières* in order to pick up where the narrative of Corinthe left off:

> Le lecteur pressé qui s'intéresserait exclusivement dans le présent ouvrage, au roman de chevalerie, à supposer qu'il n'ait pas déjà depuis longtemps refermé son volume, peut sauter, maintenant, le passage qui suit. L'index qui occupera (qui occupe) mes dernières pages lui permettra même de le faire sans difficulté: cet amateur de joutes et de cavalcades y trouvera tout de suite l'endroit du texte où il doit reprendre, si toutefois les demoiselles éplorées, les palefrois et les armures y reparaissent jamais, ce dont je ne suis pas encore certain à l'heure actuelle. Sait-on où la structure d'une telle tapisserie peut, ou non, vous entraîner? (158)[144]

Once more, as is obvious in these remarks, Robbe-Grillet is referring to his organizing function as a narrator. What he evidently highlights in this direct reference to the *table des matières*, is the open structure, the aleatory internal organization of the narrative text. Thus, at the end of this quotation the writer openly admits that he does not know what the final tapestry of his narrative will look like. It therefore seems to the reader that the author is using the *table des matières* somewhat ironically or perversely in relation to its traditional function as a guide to the apparent "order" of the narrative. Nonetheless, this table is valuable, not only for a first time reading of the *Romanesques* trilogy during which the reader can refer to it in order to skip sections or orient her/himself, but also to arrive at a better understanding of Robbe-Grillet's narrative practice. In addition, it is a very useful guide for any rereading, helping the reader to relocate things more easily when trying to pinpoint pieces of information.

One thus has a better grasp of the *tapisserie mouvante* or "changing tapestry" and the various heterogeneous elements that are woven into it through a cursory glance at this table. For example, in *Angélique ou l'enchantement*, three different men have similiar adventures in an enchanted forest: Robbe-Grillet's father, Corinthe, and the brigadier general Simon. Since the three stories follow the same basic plot and since Robbe-Grillet tends to quickly jump from one topic to another, creating a haphazard atmosphere, it is by referring to the table that the reader is able to sort out recurring details and see the correspondances among the stories: i.e., which man encountered which woman and what were the consequences. The table can also help the reader to sift through information that is given about *Mesnil* and *Maison Noire*. The former is the house where Robbe-Grillet lives, a house that has played a large role in his life for the past twenty-five years, and the latter is the house of Corinthe, that is likewise confused with Robbe-Grillet's birthplace in Brest. Furthermore, by referring to the table, the reader is also able to pick up on the games that Robbe-Grillet creates while playing with the text. For example, the brigadier general Simon is responsible for the "beautiful prisoner" Carmina. Corinthe meets a "Manrica" in the enchanted forest. The name "Manrica" is an anagram for the name "Carmina." Finally, it is through the use of the table that one is able to quickly trace the development of the different kinds of information that the author gives, for example, about Angélique and her fictional alter ego, Angélica: "J'écris le nom d'Angélica." (8); "Une curieuse lettre d'Angélica (confusion du narrateur avec Marie-Ange?)." (61); "Réalité vécue de mes romans. Angélique." (69); "Angélique offerte à Roger." (194); "Corinthe et Angélica von Salomon. ... Enfance trop douce d'Angélica, fascination pour les châtiments. ... Corinthe exhibe le sang d'Angélica." (215); "Angélica s'engage dans la *Waffen SS*." (223); "La vraie Angélique s'appelait Arno." (237); "Complaisance d'Angélique. ... Angélique me jette un sort." (242); and "Angélique disparue." (245). Beyond the transformations of the name Angélique, the reader notices that there is confusion on the part of the narrator {"Une curieuse lettre d'Angélica (confusion du narrateur avec Marie-Ange?)"} and that he only talks about the *vraie* or "true" Angélique at the end of the text.

In conclusion, Robbe-Grillet, in creating the *Romanesques* trilogy gives us an original example of "writing the self," furnishing us, in addition, with a wide range of metacommentaries that provide a clearer idea of his conception of the "autofictional narrative." Lejeune's definition of "autobiographical space" needs obviously to be expanded in order to encompass Robbe-Grillet's use of several different writing strategies within the covers of a single text. Robbe-Grillet, who maintains that he has always produced texts in which he speaks of himself, stresses the need to formulate a "new pact" with the genre of autobiography. This includes, as we have seen, not only the identity among the author, the narrator and the protagonist, but also the imaginary double(s) of protagonist/narrator/author as well as four distinct narrative voices: one that recounts childhood memories, one that makes metacommentarries on the level of *énonciation*, one that relates the adventures of Corinthe and other fictional characters, and finally the first-person narrative voice of Corinthe. Such expansions of Lejeune's concepts of the "autobiographical pact" and of "autobiographical space" may help us as readers to understand better the function of the new structures in which Robbe-Grillet juxtaposes fragments of memories, myth, history, and theory in order to define himself and to expose his principles on writing about the self. In this juxtaposing of disparate fragments, Robbe-Grillet is able to demonstrate his belief that both a fictional work and an "autofictional narrative" are works in movement. Questions central to both types of works are principally questions of structure and not questions of meaning. Yet, the reader of the *Romanesques* trilogy, as opposed to the reader of Robbe-Grillet's *Nouveau Roman* texts, is confronted with a new kind of reading since many heterogeneous elements are combined in one structure, including the legendary stories about Corinthe -- the imaginary double of Robbe-Grillet who is given his own voice -- elaborate details of Robbe-Grillet's sexual fantasies, the use of *romans de chevalerie* or "chivalric romances," Breton legends, ghost stories, and imaginary take-offs from images and photos. The metacommentaries, especially their extensive use in *Angélique ou l'enchantement*, are just one important feature in setting up this new kind of reading. They are the means by which the author justifies and explains his work and firmly establishes the narrator's function of communication with the reader. Other new elements are the three paratextual sources of information: the *table des matières*, the back covers of each text, and the *sur-titre*, *Romanesques*. *Le Miroir qui revient*, *Angélique ou l'enchantement*, and *Les Derniers jours de Corinthe* are thus highly innovative texts that demand an active participation on the part of the reader since their many fragmentary elements create an open work whose structures are continually in movememt.

Alain Robbe-Grillet, accompagnied by his wife Catherine, attended a one-day colloquium in his honor at New York University on October 9, 1998. Also, on May 5, 1998 a Robbe-Grillet Film Festival was held at Chapman University in Orange, CA. Forthcoming is an official release of Robbe-Grillet's films on video.

Chapter Five

Conclusion

> It seems that patterns of the
> memory repeat themselves. The
> unconscious often erases experiences,
> especially if they are hurtful. Yet,
> somehow willpower may retrieve
> them. - Ingrid Kisliuk, *Unveiled
> Shadows: The Witness of a Child*[145]

The central focus of this study has been *l'écriture de soi* or "writing the self"
as demonstrated in the works of three prominent contemporary French fiction
writers: Nathalie Sarraute's *Enfance*, Marguerite Duras' *L'Amant*, and Alain Robbe-
Grillet's *Romanesques* trilogy. These texts may best be characterized as *récit
autobiographique fictif* or "autofictional narrative," and as such need to be
distinguished from what has traditionally been considered as autobiography. A
distinction also needed to be made between these texts and the *Nouveau Roman* with
which these writers have been associated. It was the purpose of this study to show
how they have developed and experimented with new techniques in their
"autofictional narratives," revolutionizing autobiographical writing and opening up
new dimensions for narrative fiction in general.

To understand better the diverse aspects of "writing the self," it was necessary to define and refine the meaning of certain terms and concepts and to examine autobiography within the framework of such related genres as confessions, memoirs, the intimate journal, and the self-portrait. A distinction was also made between autobiographical writing in general, where the principal goal is to accurately preserve and historically record facts and dates, and the autobiography of a writer-novelist for whom the act of writing and aesthetic preoccupations play a pivotal role.

In refining definitions of autobiography and related genres, a critical examination of Philippe Lejeune's work in this field was presented. It was quite apparent from the start that his definiton of autobiography as "le récit rétrospectif en prose que quelqu'un fait de sa propre existence quand il met l'accent principal sur l'histoire de sa personnalité"[146] was not able to account for recent innovations in autobiographical or "autofictional" narratives. Of particular interest in the works of Sarraute, Duras, and Robbe-Grillet were the transgressions of this kind of retrospective, chronologically oriented narrative as defined by Lejeune. All three of these authors have written fragmentary and non-chronological narratives of their lives that go beyond temporal, spatial or causal restrictions.

Since all three of these authors have broken the rules of the conventional autobiographical genre, of distinct importance for this study was Lejeune's more recent concept of *espace autobiographique* or "autobiographical space," which he introduced in 1975 to expand his previous study of autobiography (*Le Pacte autobiographique*). As the critic rightfully stresses, an identity is strictly delimited in an autobiography. However, the concept of "autobiographical space" provides a theoretical frame for explaining how authors use different writing strategies across several works in order to accommodate the multiple levels of an identity. This newer concept thus served as the foundation for this study and was enlarged and adjusted while analyzing the innovative examples of "writing the self" in the works of Sarraute, Duras, and Robbe-Grillet. For example, in Sarraute's *Enfance*, the reader's focus is from the very start on the metatextual; instead of presenting the protagonist, the work opens with a dialogue between two voices. The entire narrative progresses in dialogic form. Yet, Sarraute's way of writing is very effective since the questions posed by the voice of the alter ego have multiple functions: 1.) they are metacommentaries on the story being told and force the voice of the author-narrator to become more accurate in its memory process; 2.) they initiate the reader into the innovative writing practice; and 3.) they foreground the protagonist-as-author.

In Duras' case, although *L'Amant* appears as part of the continuum of her "autofictional narratives," it is clear from both the text in question and detailed interviews that in *L'Amant*, she had developed a new form of writing, *l'écriture courante*. *L'Amant* is an "autofictional narrative" that can not be reduced to a simple novel or pure fiction since Duras creates shifts in the narrative voice by alternating between first-person and two types of third-person narration. Like Sarraute's dialoguing voices, Duras' first-person narration shows how the nature of memory itself is under interrogation and, like Sarraute's voice of the author-narrator trying to remember, will justify and defend the autobiographical memory process.

Robbe-Grillet, as Sarraute and Duras do, experiments with several writing techniques; in fact, as the *Romanesques* series progresses from *Le Miroir qui revient* to *Angélique ou l'enchantement* and to *Les Derniers jours de Corinthe*, he introduces more and more complex techniques. He has always used abrupt transitions in his narratives as well as fragmentation of the narrative voice and of the character's consciousness. However, his *Romanesques* series, as opposed to his earlier works, includes both fictional and non-fictional material, as is explicitly stated in the many metacommentaries included within the body of the text itself. Before the *Romanesques* series, a clear demarcation could be made between Robbe-Grillet's creative work and his critical work. But now, in the *Romanesques* trilogy, the writer juxtaposes fragments of memories, myth, history, and critical theory -- in order to define himself and to expose his principles as a person and a writer. It is quite clear, as Robbe-Grillet himself points out in *Angélique ou l'enchantement*, that the *Romanesques* series does not respect Lejeune's "autobiographical pact." However, the reader is led to wonder if he is aware of, or would still be unhappy with,

Lejeune's concept of "autobiographical space," since this concept allows for all the multiple levels of an identity to be shown through a diversity of narrators and characters.

In refining the concept of "autobiographical space," various kinds of paratextual information, as, for instance, detailed interviews of the author, were taken into consideration, particularly when they contained information that could affect the reader's interpretation of the particular author's work. Since all three of the authors studied here go beyond conventional writing practices such paratextual information was exceedingly useful. In this study, detailed interviews of all three authors were examined and as "paratexts," they were considered as another text in the author's "autobiographical space." Important to the study of *Enfance* is the fact that Sarraute believes that all autobiographies are fake, and that her recent writing, like *Enfance*, is still a continuation of her research on *tropismes* or "tropisms," the interior movements at the borders of our consciousness. We as readers thus realize that the most significant objective for Sarraute is to render the sensations rather than the events from her childhood.

For Duras, *L'Amant de la Chine du nord* was the means by which she was able to return to being a novelist, as she clearly stated in the book's preface. Yet, one also wonders why there was this need to write a new version of the story of the lover. This is the kind of information disclosed in interviews. For example, it is thanks to a detailed interview between Duras and Leslie Garis that we learn that she was not happy with a film version of *L'Amant* by Jean-Jacques Annaud and that this is what originally prompted her to write *L'Amant de la Chine du nord*.

Robbe-Grillet's critical theories in the *Romanesques* trilogy often contain, or are reinforced by, comments he has made in detailed interviews. Furthermore, he reiterates, especially in the long theoretical section of *Angélique ou l'enchantement*, much of what he has already said or published. For example, he repeatedly refers to how he discovered what was expected of a "true or traditional novelist" and, in turn, how he came to realize his main objective for the *Nouveau Roman*. We as readers are then able to compare paratextual information with theoretical metacommentaries that are inscribed directly in his texts. In addition, in the case of Robbe-Grillet, another noteworthy source of paratextual information is his *table des matières* in the *Romanesques* trilogy. The table serves not simply as an index by which one is able to orient oneself, but highlights in a flagrant way the many heterogeneous elements that constitute these texts. Similarly, the *sur-titre Romanesques* and the information on the back cover of each text serve the important function of forewarning the reader that the texts included in this series are neither autobiographical nor novelistic in form and that they transgress conventional genre boundaries.

In expanding the concept of "autobiographical space," it was important to study how the autobiographical story was narrated, to pay particular attention to the choice of voice and point of view, since it is their combination that makes up the new narrative situation. While examining the texts of Sarraute, Duras, and Robbe-Grillet it is advantageous to consider the narrative process as divided into *énonciation* and *énoncé*: a narrator, at the level of *énonciation*, will draw attention to the here and now of the present state of consciousness and of the writing process instead of continuing with the narration of the story (the *énoncé*). When comparing *Enfance* and *L'Amant*, one notices that in both texts direct discourse will be used. More important yet, Sarraute, Duras, and Robbe-Grillet have all introduced an alter ego in their texts, which permitted them to expand the possibilities of their writing strategies through a greater choice of voice and point of view and more flexibility to slide in and out of different narrative situations.

Of particular interest, in the study of all three authors, have been the diverse functions of the voice of the alter ego(s). In various ways, the alter ego heightens the reader's awareness of the process of recollection and new ways of writing about it. For example, in *Enfance*, the voice of the alter ego is engaged in an interior conversation with the voice of the author-narrator trying to remember and with the voice of the child Natacha. Equally complex as the use of three voices in *Enfance* is the alternation of the three types of narration in *L'Amant*. The contrast between the first-person narration and the two types of third-person narration allows Duras to present two doubles or alter egos of the author-identified narrator that are indicated simply by the indefinite *elle* or "she." Furthermore, the use of first-person narration by the author-identified narrator remembering her adolescence enables Duras to present an omniscient narrator who is capable of shifting from one period to another, from one place to another. This technique thus provides her with a means of distancing herself from her text without, on the other hand, letting fiction go free. In the *Romanesquess* trilogy, Robbe-Grillet introduces the phantasmic character of Henri de Corinthe as his chameleon alter ego or double in both life and literature. It is largely by means of this fictional character that the author is able to explore *l'imaginaire* and to delve further into his sexual fantasies, as well as his political and aesthetic views. It is useful to recall here Robbe-Grillet's claim that "J'ai formulé un pacte nouveau. C'est l'imaginaire qui parle; l'imaginaire parle du souvenir,"[147] since it helps the reader to better understand the achievements not only of Robbe-Grillet himself but also other endeavors of "autofictional narratives," like the texts of Sarraute and Duras studied here. Robbe-Grillet is right in insisting on a new definition of the "autobiographical pact," one that includes the identity among the author, the narrator, the protagonist, and the imaginary double(s) of protagonist/narrator/author.

Looking back, it is now apparent that the concept of "autobiographical space" as defined here is a form of intertextuality. This became more evident as comparisons were made between several works of each authors to see what new techniques were developed in writing the self. In Duras' case, it was especially significant to examine how she writes and rewrites the same story at various stages in her life. For example, *Un Barrage contre le Pacifique*, *Des Journées entières dans les arbres*, *l'Eden cinéma*, *L'Amant*, and *L'Amant de la Chine du nord* all recount similar events. It was particularly eye-opening to examine closely how the same experience was retold in different ways and how by retelling the same event in various works, Duras has achieved different ways of making sense of her life.

Sarraute, Duras, and Robbe-Grillet all employ metacommentaries in their "autofictional narratives" in order to reveal their attitude toward the story they are recounting and to alert the reader to the type of narrative form they are using. The most prominent characteristic of the *Romanesques* trilogy is the constant and intrusive metacommentaries that Robbe-Grillet makes on the problematic nature of his texts. His straightforward metacommentaries are similar in function to Sarraute's dialoguing voices, which comment on the autobiographical writing process, and to Duras' less self-conscious use of first-person narration that, by reaffirming details, shows that the nature of memory itself is under interrogation. All three authors' use of metacommentaries gives the reader the impression of participating in the making of the text.

By expanding Lejeune's concept of "autobiographical space," we as readers are able to understand how Sarraute, Duras and Robbe-Grillet use several different writing strategies all within the covers of a single text. Their examples of "writing the self" are clearly not pure autobiographies, since they all do away with using traditional methods and since they blur the distinction between genres. The baffled reader might well ask to what extent these "autofictional narratives" are autobiographical or fictional. There is, of course, no clear-cut answer. Sarraute, as always, is striving to render sensations or tropisms. Although the framework of the text has changed from fictional to "autofictional," it seems to me that her approach to analyzing tropisms remains the same. Duras created an imaginary photograph as the basis for her "autofictional narrative" and it is impossible for the reader to know where exactly the dividing line is between other invented details and direct autobiographical references. Robbe-Grillet blatantly introduces a fictional alter ego as a means of exploring his past, his personality, and his writing. Yet, what is obvious is that for these authors, exploration of the self became a function of writing and the self became a function of exploring writing. The most diverse writing strategies were used as a means of self-exploration and new changes in writing developed as different aspects of the self were examined.

The recent works of Sarraute, Duras, and Robbe-Grillet bring into focus new ways of looking at the world, the self, and the literary text by forcing us to question conventional boundaries. From the reader's point of view, there is no longer a clear demarcation between fact and fiction, world and text. The juxtapostion of different frames of reference inevitably gives rise to a different reading context. Sarraute, Duras, and Robbe-Grillet have definitely changed the face of autobiographical writing and it remains to be seen how their works will have an influence on the writing of "autofictional narratives" in the twenty-first century.

[1]C.D.E. Tolkin, *Andre Gide and the Art of Autobiography:* A Study of "Si le grain ne meurt" (Toronto: The macmillan Company of CanadaLimited, 1975) 10.

[2]Philippe Lejeune, *Moi aussi* (Paris: Éditions du Seuil, 1986) 18.

[3]Georges May, *L'Autobiographie* (Paris: Presses Universitaires de France, 1979) 41, my italics.

[4]Roy Pascal, *Design and Truth in Autobiography* (London: Routledge and Kegan Paul, 1960) 5.

[5]Paul Ricoeur, "Life: A Story in Search of a Narrator," *Facts and Values: Philosophical Reflections from Western and Non-Western Perspectives*, eds. M.C. Doeser and J.N. Kraay (Dordrecht, The Netherlands: Martinus Nijhoff Publishers, 1986) 129.

[6]May 150-151.

[7]Marguerite Duras, in an interview with *Le Nouvel Observateur* 57 (le 28 septembre 1984): 52.

[8]Michel Beaujour, *Miroirs d'encre: rhétorique de l'autoportrait* (Paris: Éditions du Seuil, 1980) 8.

[9]Beaujour 9.

[10]Philippe Lejeune, *L'Autobiographie en France* (Paris: Armand Colin, 1971) 14.

[11]Philippe Lejeune, *Le Pacte autobiographique* (Paris: Éditions du Seuil, 1975) 26.

[12]Lejeune, *Le Pacte autobiographique* 165.

[13]Lejeune, *Le Pacte autobiographique* 167-168.

[14]Merle Rubin, "Revealing Nonstory on Nature of Self-Love," *Christian Science Monitor* 9 April 1991: 15.

[15]Michael Sheringham, "*Ego redux*? Strategies in New French Autobiography," *Dalhousie French Studies* 17 (Special Issue: Fall-Winter 1989): 28.

[16]Inge Crosman Wimmers, *Poetics of Reading: Approaches to the Novel* (Princeton, NJ: Princeton UP, 1988) 6.

[17]For a comprehensive review of intertextuality, see Jonathan Culler, "Presupposition and Intertextuality," in *The Pursuit of Signs: Semiotics, Literature, Deconstruction* (Ithaca, NY: Cornell UP, 1981). For an expanded definition of intertextuality that includes both works that precede or

follow a particular work in question, see Michael Riffaterre, "La trace de l'intertexte," *La Pensée* 215 (octobre 1980): 4-18: "L'intertextualité est la perception, par le lecteur, de rapports entre une oeuvre et d'autres, *qui l'ont précédée ou suivie.* Ces autres oeuvres constituent l'intertexte de la première. La perception de ces rapports est donc une des composantes fondamentales de la littérarité d'une oeuvre, car cette littérarité tient à la double fonction, cognitive et esthétique, du texte." (4, my italics.)

[18]Pascal A. Ifri, "Focalisation et récits autobiographiques: l'exemple de Gide," *Poétique* (novembre 1987): 483-495.

[19]Gérard Genette, *Figures III* (Paris: Éditions du Seuil, 197) 206.

[20]Genette elaborates on the autobiographical narrator: "La seule focalisation que le narrateur autobiographique ait à respecter se définit par rapport à son information présente de narrateur et non par rapport à son information passée de héros. Il *peut*, s'il le souhaite, choisir cette seconde forme de focalisation, mais il n'y est nullement tenu, et l'on pourrait aussi bien considérer ce choix, quand il est fait, comme une paralipse, puisque le narrateur, pour s'en tenir aux informations détenues par le héros au moment de l'action, doit supprimer toutes celles qu'il a obtenues par la suite, et qui sont bien souvent capitales." [Genette, *Figures III* 214.]

[21]Pascal 177.

[22]For further information on Genette's definition of narrative situation, see: Gérard Genette, *Nouveau discours du récit* (Paris: Éditions du Seuil, 1983) 28-29.

[23]Dorrit Cohn, *Transparent Minds: Narrative Modes for Presenting Consciousness in Fiction* (Princeton, NJ: Princeton UP, 1978) 14. N.B. French linguists and, after them, literary structuralists use the term "style indirect libre" to denote what Cohn calls "narrated monologue."

[24]Cohn 14.

[25]Cohn 14-15.

[26]Following Genette's patterns, there are three types of speech in narrative fiction: 1.) "le discours narrativisé ou raconté"; 2.) "le discours transposé": a.) "style indirect" and b.) "style indirect libre"; and 3.) "le discours rapporté" or "le discours direct". For a complete discussion of the three types of speech in narrative fiction see: Genette, *Figures III* 191-194. For a further discussion on free indirect speech or discourse, see Boris A. Uspensky, *A Poetics of Composition; the Structure of the Artistic Text and Typology of a Compositional Form*, trans. Valentia Zavarin and Susan Wittig (Berkeley: U of California Press, 1973) 34-43. Uspensky distinguishes between two types of discourse rendered in the seemingly indirect style: i.) the "quasi direct discourse" where the character's speech will infiltrate into the narrator's speech; and ii.) the "narrated monologue" where the narrator's speech will dominate over the character's speech such that the narrator has reworked and edited the character's speech. (N.B. What Uspensky refers to as "quasi-direct discourse," Cohn defines as "narrated monologue.")

[27]Uspensky 32.

[28]Raylene O'Callaghan, "The Art of the (Im)Possible: The Autobiography of the French New Novelists," *Australian Journal of French Studies* 25.1 (1988): 80. Robbe-Grillet's claim in this quotation was made in *Libération, Entretien* le 17 janvier 1985: 28.

[29]Crosman Wimmers 11-12. See also: Gérard Genette, *Fiction et diction* (Paris: Éditions du Seuil, 1991) and Michael Riffaterre, *Fictional Truth* (Baltimore, MD: The Johns Hopkins UP, 1990).

[30]Gérard Genette, "The Proustian Paratexte," *SubStance* 56 (1988): 76.

[31]Genette, *Seuils* (Paris: Éditions du Seuil, 1987) 329.

[32]For Sarraute, tropisms are made of interior movements that are found at the borders of our consciousness and are the movements that come before as well as prepare our words and actions.

[33]Alain Robbe-Grillet, *Le Miroir qui revient* (Paris: Éditions de Minuit, 1984) 16-17.

[34]Nathalie Sarraute, *Enfance* (Paris: Éditions Gallimard {Collection Folio}, 1983) 38.

[35]Marguerite Duras, *L'Amant* (Paris: Éditions de Minuit, 1984) 21.

[36]I have used the term "creative catalyst" in order to distinguish between the imaginary photograph that served as the catalyst for Duras' autobiographical writing process in *L'Amant* and the telephone call from Duras' Northern Chinese lover that was the catalyst for her need to write *L'Amant*, as she explains at the end of *L'Amant*.
[37]Preface to: Nathalie Sarraute, *Portrait d'un inconnu* (Paris: Éditions Gallimard {Collection Folio}, 1956) 13.

[38]Viviane Forrester, "Portrait de Nathalie," *Magazine Littéraire* juin 1983: 19.

[39]Jason Weiss, *Writing at Risk: Interviews in Paris With Uncommon Writers* (Iowa City: U of Iowa Press, 1991) 164. These interviews were conducted in French and then translated by the author. In his introduction, Weiss explains: "All but two of the interviews were conducted in French; one of Gysin's first languages was English, and Fuentes too had learned English as a child. The rest of the pieces were translated by me at the same time that I transcribed them from the tapes. That is, I chose to translate their speech as I heard it, rather than the words on a page. In this way, I hope the flavor of their spoken language is better retained." (Weiss XV.)

[40]Alfred Cismaru, "Conversation with Nathalie Sarraute," *Telescope* 4.2 (Spring 1985): 21. This interview was also conducted in French and then translated by the author. In his preface, Cismaru accounts for the uneven flow of the interview: "The following are excerpts from a day-long conversation, or dialogue-monologue in which interviewer and interviewed engaged. Much had to be left out because of space limitations and because mechanic transcritpion, like that made by memory, never really does justice to the pauses, the hesitations, the language spoken by the eyes and by the hands, the unsaid." [Cismaru 18.]

[41]Weiss 164.

[42]Gretchen R. Besser, "Colloque avec Nathalie Sarraute, le 22 avril 1976," *The French Review* L.2 (December 1976): 284.

[43]Alison Finch and David Kelley, "Propos sur la technique du roman: Nathalie Sarraute interviewée par Alison Finch et David Kelley," *French Studies* 39 (1985): 311.

[44]Nathalie Sarraute, *L'Ère du soupçon* (Paris: Éditions Gallimard {Collection Folio}, 1956) 9. All future references to *L'Ère du soupçon* will be made to this same edition.

[45]Finch and Kelley 305.

[46]Finch and Kelley 307.

[47]Raylene O'Callaghan "The Art of the (Im)Possible: The Autobiography of the French New Novelists," *Australian Journal of French Studies* 25.1 (1988): 76.

[48]For a complete explanation of Beaujour's definition, see p. 4 of introductory chapter.

[49]Philippe Lejeune, in his article "Paroles d'enfance," directs attention to the fact that only three or four vague allusions are made to Sarraute's activity as a writer and that the rare notations concerning the adult Sarraute are linked to anamnesis or the voluntary recalling to mind of the past: "Le livre ne contient que trois ou quatre allusions à son activité d'écrivain (pages 7 - 9, 85, 213, 226 ...), allusions des plus vagues. Aucun élément d'autoportrait. Les rares notations concernant l'adulte sont liées à l'anamnèse: de son passé il lui reste une certaine répulsion pour les fraises (page 46), des cicatrices sur le bras (page 224)." [Philippe Lejeune, "Paroles d'enfance," *Revue des Sciences Humaines* 217 (janvier-mars 1990): 29.]

[50]Pascal Ifri gives a good résumé of what happens when dialogues occur in an autobiography:
> Il ne faut pas en effet oublier que ce qui est vrai pour le romancier ne l'est pas pour l'autobiographie: comme le texte du premier ne renvoie à aucune réalité, il peut contenir des dialogues représentant le point de vue de mille personnes différentes sans que le lecteur trouve quoi que ce soit à redire puisqu'en ouvrant le livre, il accepte de jouer le jeu de la fiction. Toutefois, ce n'est pas le cas de l'autobiographe qui, elle, renvoie à la réalité: en ayant recours au dialogue, son auteur prend le risque de donner un côté romanesque à son oeuvre. [Pascal A. Ifri, "Focalisation et récits autobiographiques: l'exemple de Gide," *Poétique* 72 (novembre 1987): 493-494.]

[51]There are scenes where the voice of the author-narrator trying to remember will, on its own, recount a past event. For example, see pp. 177-179.

[52]Michael Sheringham, "*Ego redux*? Strategies in New French Autobiography," *Dalhousie French Studies* 17, Special Issue (Fall - Winter 1989): 30.

[53]Nathalie Sarraute, *Enfance* (Paris: Éditions Gallimard {Collection Folio}, 1983) 7. All future references to *Enfance* will be made to this same edition.

[54]This metacommentary functions on the level of *énonciation*. I will later give a detailed description of how the narrative process is divided into *énonciation* and *énoncé*.

[55]Weiss 166.

[56]Cismaru 21.

[57]Lejeune, "Paroles d'enfance" 35.

[58]See Raylene O"Callaghan, "La nouvelle autobiographie de Nathalie Sarraute et la question du sexe du texte," Forthcoming in *Degré Second*, where O'Callaghan presents the viewpoints of various critics on the gender-marking in *Enfance*.

[59]Simone Benmussa, *Nathalie Sarraute: Qui êtes-vous?* (Lyon: La Manfacture, 1987) 139.

[60]Raylene O'Callaghan, "Voice(s) in Nathalie Sarraute's *Enfance*," *New Zealand Journal of French Studies* Special Issue (1989): 91.

[61]Paul Ricoeur, *Temps et récit, tome II: la configuration du temps dans le récit de fiction* (Paris: Éditions du Seuil, 1984) 97.

[62]Bruno Vercier, "(Nouveau) Roman et Autobiographie: *Enfance* de Nathalie Sarraute," *French Literature Series* 12 (1985): 165.

[63]Leah D. Hewitt, *Autobiographical Tiightropes* (Lincoln: U of Nebraska Press, 1990) 73-74.

[64]I am using the term "real mother" since Sarraute explains several times with great care the sensitive nature of the relationship between the child Natacha and her own mother and how her mother was resentful of the relationship between Natacha and her stepmother Véra.

[65]With the exceptions of "je ne sais" and "j'y retrouve" the past tense is used. This deviation is explained by the fact the voice of the author-narrator trying to remember is in the present of the *énonciation*, whereby it is also in the act of remembering the past.

[66]Vercier 165.

[67]Valerie Minogue, "Fragments of a Childhood: Nathalie Sarraute's *Enfance*," *Romance Studies* 9 (1986): 73.

[68]I would like to point out that the technique of reproducing and highlighting particular word phrases associated with painful and wounding situations occurs also in Proust's work. For example, when Swann confronts Odette about whether or not she had had affairs with Mme. Verdurin or with other women, Odette indignantly replies: "'Mais je n'en sais rien, moi, s'écria-t-elle avec colère, peut-être il y a très longtemps, sans me rendre compte de ce que je faisais, peut-être deux ou trois fois'" [Marcel Proust, *Du côté de chez Swann* (Paris: Éditions Gallimard {Collection Folio}, 1987) 357.] The words "deux ou trois fois" inflict a great deal of pain on Swann as is reflected in the text immediately following Odette's response: "Swann avait envisagé toutes les possibilités. La réalité

est donc quelque chose qui n'a aucun rapport avec les possibilités, pas plus qu'un coup de couteau que nous recevons avec les légers mouvements des nuages au-dessus de notre tête, puisque ces mots 'deux ou trois fois', marquèrent à vif une sorte de croix dans son coeur. Chose étrange que ces mots 'deux ou trois fois', rien que des mots, des mots prononcés dans l'air, à distance, puissent ainsi déchirer le coeur comme s'ils le touchaient véritablement, puissent rendre malade, comme un poison qu'on absorberait." [Proust 357.]

[69]For example, the "aussi liquide qu'une soupe" phrase reminds me of the words that my father would use during dinner of our childhood, when he would say to us (to my brothers, to my sister, and to me): "You can stay there all night, but you can't move until your plate is completely clean." I have forgotten the number of times when, seated at the table, I looked at peas or carrots until nine or ten o'clock at night. The words "until your plate is completely clean" will be forever engraved in my memory.

[70]Sarraute has done detailed studies on word phrases that are used figuratively so as to put abstract notions into concrete form. See, for example, *L'Usage de la parole* (Paris: Éditions Gallimard {Collection Folio}, 1980.) and *Tu ne t'aimes pas* (Paris: Éditions Gallimard, 1989.). Particularily noteworthy is her discussion of *bonheur* or "happiness" in *Tu ne t'aimes pas* (47-70).

[71]Finch and Kelley 308.

[72]Besser 284.

[73]See p. 49 and p. 104 of *Enfance*.

[74]Marcelle Marini, "Une femme sans aveu," *L'ARC* 98 (1985): 12.

[75]Carlin Romano, "Why does everyone seem to love 'The Lover'?," *Philadelphia Inquirer*, 18 April 1989: Book Section.

[76]Leah D. Hewitt, *Autobiographical Tightropes* (Lincoln: U of Nebraska Press, 1990) 98. Hewitt places "own" in quotation marks since Duras insists "that a point of view is always relative to others and is itself split and mobile, rather than a fixed property of the self." [Hewitt 98.]

[77]Carol J. Murphy, "Duras' *L'Amant*: Memories from an Absent Photo," *Remains to be Seen: Essays on Marguerite Duras*, ed. Sanford Scribner Ames (New York: Peter Lang Publishing, Inc., 1988) 173.

[78]Cohn 14.

[79]Marguerite Duras, *L'Amant* (Paris: Éditions de Minuit, 1984) 9. All future references to *L'Amant* will be made to this same edition.

[80]In *L'Amant*, Duras claims she was fifteen and a half when she met her lover. She contradicts this in *L'Amant de la Chine du nord*, where she states she was only fourteen. See p. 11 of *L'Amant* and p. 192 of *L'Amant de la Chine du nord*.

[81]Murphy 173.

[82]It is to the narratee that the narrator speaks directly and through whom the narrator demonstrates her or his communicative function. It is important not to confuse the narratee with the real reader, the potential or virtual reader, or the ideal reader. The functions of the narratee are to serve as a relay between the narrator and the reader (a function of mediation); and to be a part of the narrative discourse. The relationship between the narrator and the narratee can emphasize a theme, advance the story, and reveal the fundamental ideas or attitudes expressed in the work.

[83]Hewitt 98.

[84]Margaret Sankey, "Time and Autobiography in *L'Amant* by Marguerite Duras," *Australian Journal of French Studies*, 25.1 (1988): 66.

[85]Sankey 66.

[86]Hewitt 113.

[87]When discussing the degree of difficulty of her books with Jérôme Beaujour in *La Vie matérielle*, Duras thus comments on the reader's role: "Mes livres sont-ils difficiles, c'est ça que vous voulez savoir? Oui, ils sont difficiles. Et faciles. *L'Amant*, c'est très difficile. *La Maladie de la mort*, c'est difficile, très difficile. *L'Homme atlantique*, c'est très difficile, mais c'est si beau que ce n'est pas difficile. Même si on ne comprend pas. On ne peut pas comprendre d'ailleurs ces livres-là. Ce n'est pas le mot. Il s'agit d'une relation privée, entre le livre et le lecteur. On se plaint et on pleure, ensemble." [Marguerite Duras, *La Vie matérielle* (Paris: P.O.L., 1987) 119-120.]

Futhermore, Irène Oore speaks about Duras' ideal reader: "Le lecteur idéal est celui qui ressentant devant le texte un amour comparable à une profonde passion religieuse, le porte par sa voix au-delà du monde quotidien, au-delà du profane, vers une vérité sacrée et rituelle où tout jeu est superflu. C'est alors que 'nous trouvons ces champs sonores créés comme chaque fois pour la première fois, prononcés jusqu'à la résonance du mot, le son qu'il a, jamais entendu dans la vie courante' [Duras, *La Vie matérielle* 14-15.]. Le fait que ces champs sonores soient créés 'chaque fois pour la première fois' témoigne précisément de l'importance du lecteur, du 'vous'." [Irène Oore, "*La Vie matérielle* de Marguerite Duras, 'aller-et-retour entre moi et moi, entre vous et moi': Réflexions sur le mouvement du texte," *Dalhousie French Studies* 17, Special Issue (Fall - Winter 1989): 51.]

[88]Gerald Prince, in his article "Introduction à l'étude du narrataire," writes of the importance of the role of the narratee: "Le narrataire est un des éléments fondamentaux de toute narration. L'examen approfondi de ce qu'il représente, l'étude d'une oeuvre narrative en tant qu'elle constitue une série de signaux qui lui sont adressés, peut conduire à une lecture bien définie et à une caractérisation plus poussée de cette oeuvre. ... Elle peut permettre, en outre, de mieux apprécier le fonctionnement d'un récit et même de mieux juger de son succès au point du vue technique." [Gerald Prince, "Introduction à l'étude du narrataire," *Poétique* 14 (1973): 196.]

[89]Aliette Armel, "Le jeu autobiographique," *Magazine Littéraire* 278 (juin 1990): 28.

[90]Duras, *La Vie matérielle* 88.

[91]Duras, in an interview with *Le Nouvel Observateur* 57 (le 28 septembre 1984): 52.

---

[92]Armel 28.

[93]Armel 28.

[94]Duras, in an interview with *Le Nouvel Observateur* 52.

[95]Duras, in an interview with *Le Nouvel Observateur* 54.

[96]Armel 29.

[97]Marguerite Duras, *L'Amant de la Chine du nord* (Paris: Éditions Gallimard, 1991) 11. All future references to *L'Amant de la Chine du nord* will be made to this same edition.

[98]Leslie Garis, "The Life and Loves of Marguerite Duras," *The New York Times Magazine* 20 October 1991, Section 6: 46.

[99]For more information pertaining to the bitter feud between Duras and Annaud, see Julian Nundy, "The Duel for a Lover," *The Independent on Sunday* 26 January 1992: 26. Also, see Sylvie Genevoix, "L'amant du box-office: Jean-Jacques Annaud interviewé," *Madame Figaro* le 18 janvier 1992: 35.

[100]Daniel Toscan du Plantier, "S'aimer à Saigon," *Le Figaro Magazine* le 25 janvier 1992: 92.

[101]Suzette A. Henke, *Shattered Subjects: Trauma and Testimony in Women's Life-Writing* (New York: St. Martin's Press, 1999) XII

[102]Duras, in an interview with *Le Nouvel Observateur* 52.

[103]Hewitt 123.

[104]Marguerite Duras, *Des Journées entières dans les arbres* (Paris: Éditions Gallimard, 1954) 28. All future references to *Des Journées entières dans les arbres* will be made to this same edition.

[105]Quoted by Genette, "The Proustian Paratexte," *SubStance* 56 (1988): 75-76.

[106]Jacques Henric, "Alain Robbe-Grillet, l'enchanteur," *Art Press* (February 1988): 42.

[107]In *Angélique ou l'enchantement*, pp. 158-215 are pure metacommentary. The effect of this extensive metacommentary on the reader and Robbe-Grillet's reasons for switching from narrating to commenting as a theorist will be discussed later in this chapter.

[108]Ben Stoltzfus, in his article "The Language of Autobiography and Fiction: Gide, Barthes, and Robbe-Grillet," explains: "Gide's formula for successful fiction, using a botanical metaphor, was to compare the creative process to the flowering of a plant. The idea was to plant the seed, observe the growth, and snuff out all but the terminal buds. This procedure guaranteed the blooming of a monstrous flower, a blooming that is an excrescence, one that Gide compares to the classical artistic idea of catharsis. By cultivating an aspect of the self that bothers you the most, said Gide, you rid

yourself of it in the process." [Ben Stoltzfus, "The Language of Autobiography and Fiction: Gide, Barthes, and Robbe-Grillet," *The International Fiction Review* 15.1 (1988): 4.]

[109]Denis Roche, "Alain Robbe-Grillet, fourbe magnifique," *Magazine Littéraire* (janvier 1985).

[110]Henric 41. Thus we learn from this critic's review of *Angélique ou l'enchantement* that after its publication, the *sur-titre Romanesques* was given to the trilogy.

[111]Back cover of *Le Miroir qui revient* (Paris: Éditions de Minuit, 1984). All future references to *Le Miroir qui revient* will be made to this same edition.

[112]Jean-Pierre Salgas, "R-G: 'Je n'ai jamais parlé d'autre chose que de moi," *Magazine Littéraire* (janvier 1985).

[113]Mireille Calle-Gruber, "Quand le Nouveau Roman prend les risques du romanesque," *Autobiographie et biographie: colloque franco-allemand de Heidelberg*, eds. Mireille Calle-Gruber and Arnold Rothe (Paris: Librairie A.-G. Nizet, 1989) 188.

[114]Calle-Gruber 188.

[115]It is interesting to note that Robbe-Grillet begins the reflection on his youth with the study of the mysterious character of Henri de Corinthe. A detailed analysis of Henri de Corinthe, the alter ego in literature of Robbe-Grillet, is provided later in this chapter.

[116]As with the metacommentaries made by Sarraute and Duras, Robbe-Grillet's metacommentaries are made at the level of *énonciation*. This is the level at which the author draws attention to the present state of the writing process and the author-narrator's personal point of view.

[117]Michel Rybalka, "Alain Robbe-Grillet: At Play With Criticism," *Three Decades of the French New Novel*, ed. Lois Oppenheim (Chicago: U of Illinois Press, 1986) 40-41.

[118]Oppenheim, ed., *Three Decades of the French New Novel* 24. Oppenheim and Evelyne Costa de Beauregard translated this collection of presentations made at the 1982 colloquium on the *Nouveau Roman* at New York University.

[119]See *Pour un nouveau roman*, where Robbe-Grillet already insisted on the reader's active role. Particularly noteworthy is the chapter "Nouveau roman, homme nouveau" where he writes about the errors of the critics in their understanding of the *Nouveau Roman*: "La voici donc cette charte du Nouveau Roman telle que la rumeur publique la colporte: 1.) Le Nouveau Roman a codifié les lois du roman futur. 2.) Le Nouveau Roman a fait table rase du passé. 3.) Le Nouveau Roman veut chasser l'homme du monde. 4.) Le Nouveau Roman vise à la parfaite objectivité. 5.) Le Nouveau Roman, *difficilement lisible, ne s'adresse qu'aux spécialistes*." [Alain Robbe-Grillet, *Pour un nouveau roman* (Paris: Éditions de Minuit {Collection "Critique"}, 1961) 114, my italics.]

[120]Jean Montalbetti, "Alain Robbe-Grillet, autobiographe," *Magazine Littéraire* (janvier 1985): propos recueillis.

[121]O'Callaghan, "The Art of the (Im)Possible: The Autobiography of the French New

Novelists" 80.

[122]Oppenheim, ed., *Three Decades of the French New Novel* 27.

[123]The development in *Angélique ou l'enchantement* of two first-person narrative subjects will be discussed later in this chapter.

[124]I place "chapters" in quotation marks because all three texts are divided into what may more aptly be termed sections.

[125]Sheringham 32.

[126]Alain Robbe-Grillet, *Angélique ou l'enchantement* (Paris: Éditions de Minuit, 1987) 24-25. All future references to *Angélique ou l'enchantement* will be made to this same edition.

[127]See also p. 120 of *Angélique ou l'enchantement* for another example of this same type of narrative switch.

[128]Calle-Gruber 196.

[129]Sjef Houppermans, "Un miroir enchanté," *Dalhousie French Studies* 17, Special Issue (Fall-Winter 1989): 39.

[130]Calle-Gruber 190.

[131]Sheringham 32.

[132] Alain Robbe-Grillet, *Les Derniers jours de Corinthe* (Paris: Éditions de Minuit, 1994) 23. All future references to *Les Derniers jours de Corinthe* will be made to this same edition.

[133] See p. 87 of *Les Derniers jours de Corinthe*.

[134]See pp. 166-167 of *Le Miroir qui revient*.

[135]Calle-Gruber 192.

[136]Georges Gusdorf, "Conditions et limites de l'autobiographie," *Formen der Selbstdarstellung: Analekten zu einer Geschichte des literarischen Selbstportraits*, eds. Günther Reichenkron and Erich Hasse (Berlin: Dunker and Humblot, 1956) 117.

[137]Pascal 148.

[138]Michel Contat, "Portrait de Robbe-Grillet en châtelain," *Le Monde* vendredi le 12 février 1988: 15.

[139]For example, in *Angélique ou l'enchantement* (7-8) Robbe-Grillet writes about grimacing faces he sees in the grains of different types of wood and in the wallpaper surrounding him. He also muses about the uncertainty of the images he is using (104-109). This reflection by Robbe-Grillet, a metacommentary, leads in turn into an imaginary take-off from the symbolist painting that is in front

of him. The symbolist painting is used again when he talks about the small flower of Odenwald (127-128).

[140]In clarifying the distinction between autobiography and confessions/apology, Georges May states: "L'intention autobiographique désignée par le terme d'apologie peut se définir comme le besoin d'écrire afin de justifier en public les actions qu'on a commises ou les idées qu'on a professées. Ce besoin se fait ressentir de manière particulièrement pénible et urgent *lorsqu'on a lieu de penser qu'on a été calomnié.*" [Georges May, "*L'Autobiographie* (Paris: Presses Universitaires de France, 1979) 41, my italics.]

[141]Houppermans 38-39.

[142]Henric 43.

[143]Gérard Genette, *Seuils* (Paris: Éditions du Seuil, 1987) 292.

[144]An example of a table entry from the long theoretical section of *Angélique ou l'enchantement* is: "L'oeuvre et la théorie. Méprises sur l'être-objet. Polémique et humour. Efficacité des malentendus. Information vs. signification. Lisibilité de *Pour un Nouveau Roman*. Mes succes de conférencier. ....166." (252)

[145]Ingrid Kisliuk, *Unveiled Shadows: The Witness of a Child* (Newton, MA: Nanomir Press, 1998) 54.

[146] Lejeune, *L'Autobiographie en France* 14.

[147] O'Callaghan, "The Art of the (Im)Possible: The Autobiography of the French New Novelists" 80.

Bibliography

A. Primary Sources

Duras, Marguerite. *Un Barrage contre le Pacifique*. Paris: Éditions Gallimard (Collection Folio), 1950.

-----. *Des Journées entières dans les arbres*. Paris: Éditions Gallimard, 1954.

-----. *Moderato Cantabile*. Paris: Éditions de Minuit, 1958.

-----. *Hiroshima mon amour*. Paris: Éditions Gallimard (Collection Foliio), 1960.

-----. *L'Été 80*. Paris: Éditions de Minuit, 1980.

-----. *L'Amant*. Paris: Éditions de Minuit, 1984.

-----. *La Douleur*. Paris: P.O.L., 1985.

-----. *La Pute de la côte normande*. Paris: Éditions de Minuit, 1986.

-----. *Emily L*. Paris: Éditions de Minuit, 1987.

-----. *La Vie matérielle*. Paris: P.O.L., 1987.

-----. *L'Eden cinéma*. Paris: Actes Sud, 1988.

-----. *L'Amant de la Chine du nord*. Paris: Éditions Gallimard, 1991.

-----. *Yann Andréa Steiner*. Paris: P.O.L., 1992.

-----. *C'est tout*. Paris: Éditions de Minuit, 1995.

Robbe-Grillet, Alain. *Les Gommes*. Paris: Éditions de Minuit, 1953.

-----. *Le Voyeur*. Paris: Éditions de Minuit, 1955.

-----. *Dans le labyrinthe*. Paris: Éditions de Minuit, 1959.

-----. *Pour un nouveau roman*. Paris: Éditions de Minuit (Collection "Critique"), 1961.

-----. *La Jalousie*. Paris: Éditions de Minuit, 1967.

-----. *Pour une révolution à New York*. Paris: Éditions de Minuit, 1970.

-----. *Djinn*. Paris: Éditions de Minuit, 1981.

-----. *Le Miroir qui revient*. Paris: Édition de Minuit, 1984.

-----. *Angélique ou l'enchantement*. Paris: Éditions de Minuit, 1987.

-----. *Les Derniers jours de Corinthe*. Paris: Éditions de Minuit, 1994.

Sarraute, Nathalie. *L'Ère du soupçon*. Paris: Éditions Gallimard (Collection Folio), 1956.

140

-----. *Portrait d'un inconnu*. Paris: Éditions Gallimard (Collection Folio), 1956.

-----. *Tropismes*. Paris: Éditions de Minuit, 1957.

-----. *Le Planétarium*. Paris: Éditions Gallimard (Collection Folio), 1959.

-----. *Les Fruits d'or*. Paris: Éditions Gallimard (Collection Folio), 1963.

-----. *Vous les entendez*. Paris: Éditions Gallimard (Collection Folio), 1972.

-----. *L'Usage de la parole*. Paris: Éditions Gallimard (Collection Folio), 1980.

-----. *Enfance*. Paris: Éditions Gallimard (Collection Folio), 1983.

-----. *Tu ne t'aimes pas*. Paris: Éditions Gallimard, 1989.

-----. *Ici*. Paris: Éditions Gallimard, 1995.

-----. *Ouvrez*. Paris: Éditions Gallimard, 1997.

B. Secondary Sources

Adams, Timothy Dow. *Light Writing and Life Writing: Photography in Autobiography*. Chapel Hill: U of NC Press, 2000.

Adler, Laura. *Marguerite Duras*. Paris: Éditions Gallimard, 1999.

Ames, Sanford Scribner, ed. *Remains To Be Seen: Essays On Marguerite Duras*. New York: Peter Lang, 1988.

Angles, Daphne. "Same Time, Same Cafe." *The New York Times Book Review* 25 November 1990: 7.

Armel, Aliette. *Marguerite Duras et l'autobiographie*. Paris: Le Castor Astral, 1990.

-----. "Le jeu autobiographique." *Magazine Littéraire*. 278 (juin 1990): 28-31.

Asso, Françoise. "Avec Nathalie Sarraute." *La Quinzaine* du 1er au 15 octobre 1989: 4-7.

Assouline, Pierre. "La vraie vie de Marguerite Duras." *Magazine Lire*. (octobre 1991): 49-59.

Auster, Paul, and Lydia Davis. *Life/Situations: Essays Written and Spoken*. New York: Pantheon, 1977.

Austin, J.L. *How to Do Things With Words*. Cambridge: Harvard UP, 1975.

Bajomée, Danielle and Ralph Heyndels. *Écrire dit-elle*. Bruxelles: Éditions de l'Université de Bruxelles, 1985.

Bakhtin, M. M. *The Dialogic Imagination: Four Essays*. Austin, TX: U of Texas Press, 1981.

Beaujour, Michel. *Miroirs d'encre: rhétorique de l'autoportrait*. Paris: Éditions du Seuil, 1980.

-----. *La Cérémonie des adieux*. Paris: Éditions Gallimard (Collection Folio), 1981.

Benmussa, Simone. *Nathalie Sarraute: Qui êtes-vous?* Lyon: La Manufacture, 1987.

Besser, Gretchen Rous. "Colloque avec Nathalie Sarraute, le 22 avril 1976." *The French Review* L.2 (December 1976): 284 -289.

-----. *Nathalie Sarraute*. Boston: Twayne Publishers, 1979.

-----. "Sarraute on Childhood - Her Own." *French Literature Series* 12 (1985): 154-161.

Benveniste, Émile. *Problèmes de linguistique générale*. Paris: Éditions Gallimard, 1966.

Borgomano, Madeleine. *Duras: une lecture des fantasmes*. Paris: Cistre-Essais, 1985.

Boyer, Zoë. "French Women Writers: The Forthright Generation." *Essays in French Literature* 27 (November 1990): 64-74.

Braudeau, Michel. "Le rap de Marguerite." *Le Monde* 28 juin 1991: 18.

Bruss, Elizabeth. "L'autobiographie considérée comme acte littéraire." *Poétique* 17 (1974): 14-26.

-----. *Autobiographical Acts: The Changing Situation of a Literary Genre*. Baltimore: Johns Hopkins UP, 1976.

Calle-Gruber, Mireille. "Quand le Nouveau Roman prend les risques du romanesque." *Autobiographie et biographie: colloque franco-allemand de Heidelberg*. Eds. Mireille Calle-Gruber and Arnold Rothe. Paris: Librairie A.-G. Nizet, 1989. 185-199.

Clayton, Alan J. *Nathalie Sarraute ou le tremblement de l'écriture*. Paris: Archives des Lettres Modernes, 1989.

-----. "Coucou ... attrapez-moi ..." *Revue des Sciences Humaines* 217 (janvier-mars 1990): 9-22.

Chaigneau, Jean-François. "Marguerite Duras: Yann Andrea voulait la connaître avant de se tuer." *Paris Match* le 2 juillet 1992: 30-31.

Cismaru, Alfred. "Conversations with Nathalie Sarraute." *Telescope* 4.2 (Spring 1985): 17-24.

Cohn, Dorrit C. *Transparent Minds: Narrative Modes for Presenting Consciousness in Fiction*. Princeton: Princeton UP, 1978.

Contat, Michel. "Portrait de Robbe-Grillet en châtelain." *Le Monde* vendredi le 12 février 1988: 15.

Cordesse, Gérard. "Narration et focalisation." *Poétique* 76 (novembre 1988): 487-498.

Culler, Jonathan. *The Pursuit of Signs: Semiotic, Literature, Deconstruction*. Ithaca: Cornell UP, 1981.

Danto, Ginger. "Me, My Selves and I." *The New York Times Book Review* 25 November 1990: 7.

Doubrovsky, Serge. "Autobiographie/Vérité/Psychanalyse." *L'Esprit Créateur* XX.3 (Fall 1980): 87-97.

Duras, Marguerite. "L'inconnue de la rue Catinat - Entretien avec Marguerite Duras." *Le Nouvel Observateur* 57 (le 28 septembre 1984): 52-54.

Eakin, Paul John. *Fictions in Autobiography: Studies in the Art of Self-Invention*. Princeton: Princeton UP, 1985.

Ehrlich, Susan. *Point of View: A Linguistic Analysis of Literary Style*. New York: Routledge, 1990.

Ferney, Frédéric. "Duras l'inconsolable." *Le Nouvel Observateur* le 19 avril 1985: 68-69.

Finch, Alison, et David Kelley. "Propos sur la technique du roman: Nathalie Sarraute interviewée par Alison Finch et David Kelley." *French Studies* 39 (1985): 305-315.

Fish, Stanley E. "How to Do Things with Austin and Searle: Speech Act Theory and Literary Criticism." *Modern Language Notes* 91 (1976): 983-1025.

Fitch, Brian T. *Reflections in the Mind's Eye: Reference and its Problematization in 20th Century French Fiction*. Toronto: U of Toronto Press, 1991.

Flambard-Weisbart, Véronique. "Nathalie Sarraute and the Thought from the Outside." *UCLA French Studies* 8 (1990): 1-9.

Forrester, Viviane. "Portrait de Nathalie." Magazine Littéraire (juin 1983): 18-21.

Gallop, Jane. "French Feminism." *A New History of French Literature*. Ed. Denis Hollier. Cambridge: Harvard UP, 1989. 1045-1049.

Garis, Leslie. "The Life and Loves of Marguerite Duras." *The New York Times Magazine* 20 October 1991, sec. 6: 44-61.

Genette, Gérard. *Figures III*. Paris: Éditions du Seuil, 1972.

-----. *Palimpsestes*. Paris: Éditions du Seuil, 1982.

-----. *Nouveau discours du récit*. Paris: Éditions du Seuil, 1983.

-----. *Seuils*. Paris: Éditions du Seuil, 1987.

-----. "The Proustian Paratexte." *SubStance* 56 (1988): 63-77.

-----. "Le Statut pragmatique de la fiction narrative." *Poétique* 78 (avril 1989): 237-249.

-----. *Fiction et diction*. Paris: Éditions du Seuil, 1991.

Genevoix, Sylvie. "*L'Amant* du box-office: Jean-Jacques Annaud interviewé." *Madame Figaro* le 18 janvier 1992: 35.

Gide, André. *La Symphonie pastorale*. Paris: Éditions Gallimard (Collection Folio), 1925.

-----. *Si le grain ne meurt*. Paris: Éditions Gallimard (Collection Folio), 1955.

-----. *L'Immoraliste*. Paris: Mercure de France (Collection Folio), 1988.

Glassman, Deborah N. *Marguerite Duras: Fascinating Vision and Narrative Cure*. London and Toronto: Associated University Presses, 1991.

Golopentia, Sanda. *Les voies de la pragmatique*. Saratoga,CA: Anma Libri, 1988.

Greene, Robert W. "Nathalie Sarraute's L'Usage de la parole, or Re(en)trop(iz)ing Tropismes." *Novel: A Forum on Fiction* 16.3 (Spring 1983): 197-214.

Goux, Jean-Joseph. "Mise en Abyme." *A New History of French Literature*. Ed. Denis Hollier. Cambridge: Harvard UP, 1989. 872-876.

Gunn, Janet Varner. *Autobiography: Toward a Poetics of Experience*. Philadelphia: U of Pennsylvania Press, 1982.

Gusdorf, Georges. "Conditions et limites de l'autobiographie." *Formen der Selbstdarstellung: Analekten zu einer Geschichte des literarischen Selbstportraits*. Eds. Günther Reichenkron and Erich Haase. Berlin: Duncker and Humblot, 1956. 105-123.

-----. *Lignes de vie 2, auto-bio-graphie*. Paris: Éditions Odile Jacob, 1991.

Hart, Francis R. "Notes for an Anatomy of Modern Autobiography." *New Literary*

History: A Journal of Theory and Interpretation Spring (1970): 485-511.

Harvey, Robert and Hélène Volant. *Marguerite Duras: A Biography.* Westport, CT: Greenwood Publishers, 1999.

Heilbrun, Carolyn G. *Writing a Woman's Life.* New York: Ballantine Books, 1989.

Hébert, Pierre. "Les Narrataires du journal intime: l'exemple de Lionel Groulx." *The French Review* LIX.6 (May 1986): 849-858.

Henke, Suzette A. *Shattered Subjects: Trauma and Testimony in Women's Life-Writing.* New York: St. Martin's Press, 1998.

Henric, Jacques. "Alain Robbe-Grillet, l'enchanteur." *Art Press* (February 1988): 41-44.

Hewitt, Leah D. *Autobiographical Tightropes.* Lincoln: U of Nebraska Press, 1990.

Hofmann, Carol. *Forgetting and Marguerite Duras.* Colorado: UP of Colorado, 1991.

Houppermans, Sjef. "Un miroir enchanté." *Dalhousie French Studies* 17, Special Issue (Fall-Winter 1989): 37-45.

Ifri, Pascal A. "Focalisation et récits autobiographiques: l'exemple de Gide." *Poétique* 72 (novembre 1987): 483-495.

Iser, Wolfgang. *The Implied Reader: Patterns of Communication in Prose Fiction from Bunyan to Beckett.* Baltimore: Johns Hopkins UP, 1974.

-----. *The Act of Reading: A Theory of Aesthetic Response.* Baltimore: Johns Hopkins UP, 1978.

Jay, Paul. *Being in the Text: Self-Representation from Wordsworth to Roland Barthes.* Ithaca: Cornell UP, 1984.

Jelinek, Esther C., ed. *Women's Autobiography: Essays in Criticism.* Bloomington: Indiana UP, 1980.

Kazin, Alfred. "Autobiography as Narrative." *Michigan Quarterly Review* III.4 (1964): 210-216.

Kisliuk, Ingrid. *Unveiled Shadows: The Witness of a Child.* Newtown, MA: Nanomir Press, 1998.

Kristeva, Julia. "Women's Time." *Critical Theory Since 1965.* Eds. Hazard Adams and Leroy Searle. Tallahassee: Florida State UP, 1986. 469-484.

Lejeune, Philippe. *L'Autobiographie en France.* Paris: Armand Colin, 1971.

-----. *Le Pacte autobiographique.* Paris: Éditions du Seuil, 1975.

-----. *Moi aussi.* Paris: Éditions du Seuil, 1986.

-----. "L'Autobiocopie." *Autobiograhie et biographie: Colloque franco-allemand de Heidelberg.* Eds. Mireille Calle-Gruber et Arnold Rothe. Paris: Librairie A.-G. Nizet, 1989. 53-66.

-----. "Paroles d'enfance." *Revue des Sciences Humaines* 217 (janvier-mars 1990): 23-38.

-----. *La Mémoire et l'oblique.* Paris: P.O.L., 1991.

Loesberg, Jonathan. "Autobiography as Genre, Act of Consciousness, Text." *Prose Studies* (September 1971): 169-185.

Mathieu-Colas, Michel. "Récit et vérité." *Poétique* 80 (novembre 1989): 387-403.

May, Georges. *L'Autobiographie*. Paris: Presses Universitaires de France, 1979.

Minogue, Valerie. *Nathalie Sarraute and the War of the Words: A Study of Five Novels*. Edinburgh: Edinburgh UP, 1981.

-----. "Fragments of a Childhood: Nathalie Sarraute's Enfance." *Romance Studies* 9 (1986): 71-83.

-----. "Le Cheval de Troie. À propos de *Tu ne t'aimes pas*." *Revue des Sciences Humaines* 217 (janvier-mars 1990): 151-161.

Moi, Toril. "An Intellectual Woman in Postwar France." *A New History of French Literature*. Ed. Denis Hollier. Cambridge: Harvard UP, 1989. 982-988.

Montalbetti, Jean. "Alain Robbe-Grillet, autobiographe." *Magazine Littéraire*, propos recueillis, janvier 1985.

Mortimer, Armine Kotin. *Plotting to Kill*. New York: Peter Lang, 1991.

Nundy, Julian. "The Duel for a Lover." *The Independent on Sunday* 26 January 1992: 26.

Nussbaum, Martha. "Fictions of the Soul." *Philosophy and Literature*. 7.2 (October 1983): 145-161.

O'Callaghan, Raylene. "The Art of the (Im)Possible: The Autobiography of the French New Novelists." *Australian Journal of French Studies* 25.1 (1988): 71-91.

-----. "Reading Nathalie Sarraute's Enfance: Reflections on Critical Validity." *Romanic Review* 80.3 (May 1989): 445-461.

-----. "The Uses and Abuses of Enchantment in Robbe-Grillet's Angélique ou l'enchantement." *Dalhousie French Studies* 17, Special Issue (Fall-Winter 1989): 109-116.

-----. "Voice(s) in Nathalie Sarraute's Enfance." *New Zealand Journal of French Studies* Special Issue (1989): 83-94.

-----. "La Nouvelle autobiographie de Nathalie Sarraute et la question du sexe du texte." Forthcoming in *Degré Second*.

Olney, James, ed. *Autobiography: Essays Theoretical and Critical*. Princeton: Princeton UP, 1980.

-----. *Studies in Autobiography*. Oxford: Oxford UP, 1988.

Oore, Irène. "*La Vie matérielle* de Marguerite Duras, 'aller-et-retour entre moi et moi, entre vous et moi': Réflexions sur le mouvement du texte." *Dalhousie French Studies* 17, Special Issue (Fall-Winter 1989): 47-53.

Oppenheim, Lois, ed. *Three Decades of the French New Novel*. Chicago: U of Illinois Press, 1986.

Pauly, Rebecca M. *Le Berceau et la bibliothèque: le paradoxe de l'écriture autobiographique*. Saratoga, CA: ANMA Libri & Co., 1989.

Pascal, Roy. *Design and Truth in Autobiography*. London: Routledge and Kegan Paul, 1960.

Picard, Michel. *Lire le temps*. Paris: Éditions de Minuit, 1989.

Pierrot, Jean. *Marguerite Duras*. Paris: Librairie José Corti, 1986.

-----. *Nathalie Sarraute*. Paris: Librairie José Corti, 1990.

Pinthon, Monique. *"Émily L.*, écrire, dit-elle?" *Information Littéraire* (novembre-décembre 1988): 46-47.

Piwowarczyk, Mary Ann. "The Narratee and the Situation of Enunciation: A Reconsideration of Prince's Theory." *Genre* IX (1976): 161-177.

Prince, Gerald. "Introduction à l'étude du narrataire." *Poétique* 14 (1973): 178-196.

-----. "The Naratee Revisted." *Conference Paper: Colloquium on 20th Century Literature* 1-9.

-----. "The Nouveau Roman." *A New History of French Literature*. Ed. Denis Hollier. Cambridge: Harvard UP, 1989.

Proust, Marcel. *Contre Sainte-Beuve*. Paris: Éditions Gallimard (Collection Folio), 1954.

-----. *Du côté de chez Swann*. Paris: Éditions Gallimard (Collection Folio), 1987.

Ray, William. "Recognizing Recognition: The Intra-Textual and Extra-Textual Critical Persona." *Diacritics* (Winter 1977): 20-33.

Ricoeur, Paul. *Temps et récit, tome I: l'ordre philosophique*. Paris: Éditions du Seuil, 1983.

-----. *Temps et récit, tome II: la configuration du temps dans le récit de fiction*. Paris: Éditions du Seuil, 1984.

-----. "Life: A Story in Search of a Narrator." *Facts and Values: Philosophical Reflections from Western and Non-Western Perspectives*. Eds. M.C. Doeser and J.N. Kraay. Dordrecht, The Netherlands: Martinus Nijhoff Publishers, 1986. 121-132.

-----. "The Metaphorical Process as Cognition, Imagination, and Feeling." *Critical Theory Since 1965*. Eds. Hazard Adams and Leroy Searl. Tallahassee: Florida State UP, 1986. 423-434.

Riding, Alan. "Marguerite Duras and Thoughts of Love." *New York Times* 26 March 1990, late ed.: C11.

Riffaterre, Michael. *Semiotics of Poetry*. Bloomington: Indiana UP, 1978.

-----. "La syllepse intertextuelle." *Poétique* 40 (1979): 496-501.

-----. "La trace de l'intertexte." *La Pensée* 215 (octobre 1980): 4-18.

-----. "On the Sign Systems of Biography." *The Comparative Perspective in Literature*. Eds. Clayton Koelb and Susan Noakes. Ithaca: Cornell UP, 1988. 356-365.

-----. *Fictional Truth*. Baltimore: The Johns Hopkins UP, 1990.

Roche, Denis. "Alain Robbe-Grillet, fourbe magnifique." *Magazine Littéraire*, janvier 1985.

Romano, Carlin. "Why Does Everyone Seem to Love 'The Lover'?" *Philadelphia Inquirer* 18 April 1989: Book Section.

Ronen, Ruth. "The Semiotics of Fictional Time: Three Metaphors in the Study of Temporality in Fiction." *Style* 24.1 (Spring 1990): 22-44.

Rubin, Merle. "Revealing Nonstory on Nature of Self-Love." *Christian Science Monitor* 9 April 1991: 15.

Rykner, Arnaud. "Des Tropismes de l'acteur à l'acteur des tropismes." *Revue des*

146

Sciences Humaines 217 (janvier-mars 1990): 139-147.

Salgas, Jean-Pierre. "R-G: 'Je n'ai jamais parlé d'autre chose que de moi.'" *Magazine Littéraire* janvier 1985.

Sankey, Margaret. "Time and Autobiography in L'Amant by Marguerite Duras." *Australian Journal of French Studies* 25.1 (1988): 58-70.

Saporta, Marc, ed. *Nathalie Sarraute, L'Arc: revue trimestrielle.* Le Revest-Saint-Martin: Éditions LE JAS, 1984.

-----. Marguerite Duras. *L'Arc.* Le Revest-Saint-Martin: Éditions LE JAS, 1985.

Sartre, Jean-Paul. *La Nausée.* Éditions Gallimard (Collection Folio), 1938.

-----. *Les Mots.* Paris: Éditions Gallimard (Collection Folio), 1964.

Selous, Trista. *The Other Woman: Feminism and Femininity in the Work of Marguerite Duras.* New Haven: Yale UP, 1988.

Shapiro, Stephen A. "The Dark Continent of Literature: Autobiography." *Comparative Literature Studies* V.4 (1968): 421-454.

Sheringham, Michael. "French Autobiography: Texts, Contexts, Poetics." *Journal of European Studies* 16 (1986): 59-71.

-----. "Ego redux? Strategies in New French Autobiography." *Dalhousie French Studies* 17, Special Issue (Fall-Winter 1989): 27-35.

Slama, Béatrice. "De La 'Littérature féminine' à 'l'écrire-femme'." *Littérature* 44 (décembre 1981): 51-73.

Smith, Sidonie. *A Poetics of Women's Autobiography.* Bloomington: Indiana UP, 1987.

-----. "Self,Subject, and Resistance: Marginalities and Twentieth-Century Autobiographical Practice." *Tulsa Studies in Women's Literature* 6.1 (1990): 11-24.

Stoltzfus, Ben. "The Language of Autobiography and Fiction: Gide, Barthes, and Robbe-Grillet." *The International Fiction Review* 15.1 (1988): 3-8.

Sturrock, John. "The New Model Autobiographer." *New Literary History* 9 (1977-1978): 54-62.

Suleiman, Susan R. "The Question of Readability in Avant-Garde Fiction." *Studies in Twentieth Century Literature* 6.1 & 2 (Fall 1981 - Spring 1982): 17 - 33.

Suleiman, Susan R. and Inge Crosman, eds. *The Reader in the Text: Essays on Audience and Interpretation.* Princeton: Princeton UP, 1980.

Tadié, Jean-Yves. "Découpage et montage de La Recherche." *Magazine Littéraire* 246 (octobre 1987): 37-38.

Todd, Olivier. "Jean Paul Sartre on His Autobiography." *The Listener* 57 (June 6, 1957): 915-916.

Tolton, C.D.E. *André Gide and the Art of Autobiography: A Study of "Si le grain ne meurt."* Toronto: The Macmillan Company of Canada Limited, 1975.

Toscan du Plantier, Daniel. "S'aimer à Saigon." *Le Figaro Magazine* le 25 janvier 1992: 92.

Uspensky, Boris A. *A Poetics of Composition; the Structure of the Artistic Text and Typology of a Compositional Form.* Trans. Valentina Zavarin and Susan

Wittig. Berkeley: U of California Press, 1973.

Valdés, Mario J., ed. *A Ricoeur Reader: Reflection and Imagination.* Toronto: U of Toronto Press, 1991.

Vercier, Bruno. "(Nouveau) Roman et Autobiographie: *Enfance* de Nathalie Sarraute." *French Literature Series* 12 (1985): 162-170.

Vircondelet, Alain. *Duras: Biographie.* Paris: Éditions François Bourin, 1991.

Ward Jouve, Nicole. *White Woman Speaks With Forked Tongue: Criticism as Autobiography.* New York: Routledge, 1991.

Watson-Williams, Helen. *The Novels of Nathalie Sarraute: Towards an Aesthetic.* Amsterdam: Éditions Rodopi BV., 1981.

Waugh, Patricia. *Feminine Fictions: Revisiting the Postmodern.* New York: Routledge, 1989.

West, Paul. "A Phenomenologist Bares His Heart." *The New York Times Book Review* 27 January 1991: 24.

Weiss, Jason. *Writing at Risk: Interviews in Paris With Uncommon Writers.* Iowa City: U of Iowa Press, 1991.

Wilson, Suzanne. "Auto-bio-graphie: vers une théorie de l'écriture féminine." *The French Review* 63.4 (March 1990): 617-622.

Wimmers, Inge Crosman. *Poetics of Reading: Approaches to the Novel.* Princeton: Princeton UP, 1988.

Index

A

B

C

D

152

STUDIES IN FRENCH LITERATURE

1. Gerald Groves (trans.), **Germain Nouveau's Symbolist Poetry 1851-1920:** *Valentines*

2. Anne-Marie Brinsmead, **Strategies of Resistance in** *Les Liaisons Dangereuses***: Heroines in Search of "Author-ity"**

3. Jean-Jacques Thomas (compiler), **Concordance de** *Poemes* **by Yves Bonnefoy**

4. René Daumal, **René Daumal's** *Mugle* **and** *The Silk*, translated with an Introduction by Phil Powrie

5. Leonora Timm (trans. & ed.), **A Modern Breton Political Poet -- Anjela Duval: A Biography and An Anthology**

6. Sharon Harwood-Gordon, **The Poetic Style of Corneille's Tragedies: An Aesthetic Interpretation**

7. David Bryant, **The Rhetoric of Pessimism and Strategies of Containment in the Short Stories of Guy de Maupassant**

8. Pierre Nguyen-Van-Huy, **Le devenir et la conscience cosmique chez Saint-Expupéry**

9. Roxanne Hanney, **The Invisible Middle Term in Proust's** *A La Recherche Du Temps Perdu*

10. Michael G. Paulson, **A Critical Analysis of de La Fayette's** *La Princesse de Clèves* **as a Royal Exemplary Novel: Kings, Queens, and Splendor**

11. Jeri Debois King, **Paratextuality in Balzac's** *La Peau de Chagrin***: The Wild Ass's Skin**

12. Emil Zola, *My Hatreds/Mes Haines*, translated and with an introdution by Palomba Paves-Yashinsky and Jack Yashinsky

13. Larry W. Riggs, **Resistance to Culture in Moliére, Laclos, Flaubert, and Camus, A Post-Modernist Approach**

14. Alphonse de Lamarine, *Poetical Meditations/Méditations Poétiques*, translated and with an introduction by Gervase Hittle

15. Jehan de Paris, *The Romance of Jehan de Paris/Le Romant de Jehan de Paris*, Guy R. Mermier (trans.)

16. Gerald Macklin, **A Study of Theatrical Vision in Arthur Rimbaud's** *Illuminations*

17. Maxwell Adereth, **Elsa Triolet and Louis Aragon, An Introduction to Their Interwoven Lives and Works**

18. Christopher Todd, **A Century of French Best-Seller (1890-1990)**

19. Anne Judge and Solange Lamothe, **Stylistic Developments in Literary and Non-Literaty French Prose**